My Car in Managua

My Car in Managua

Forrest D. Colburn
Illustrations by Róger Sánchez Flores

UNIVERSITY OF TEXAS PRESS   AUSTIN

Parts of this opusculum were published in *Harper's*, Condé Nast's *Traveler*, *The New Leader*, *Caribbean Review*, and the *Princeton Alumni Weekly*.

Copyright © 1991 by the University of Texas Press
All rights reserved
Printed in the United States of America

Second paperback printing, 1993

Requests for permission to reproduce material from this work should be sent to Permissions, University of Texas Press, Box 7819, Austin, TX 78713-7819.

♾ The paper used in this publication meets the minimum requirements of American National Standard for Information Sciences—Permanence of Paper for Printed Library Materials, ANSI Z39.48-1984.

Library of Congress Cataloging-in-Publication Data

Colburn, Forrest D.
    My car in Managua / Forrest D. Colburn ; illustrations by Róger Sánchez Flores. — 1st ed.
      p.   cm.
    "Parts of this opusculum were published in Harper's, Condé Nast's Traveler, The New Leader, Caribbean Review, and the Princeton Alumni Weekly."
    ISBN 0-292-75123-0 (alk.). — ISBN 0-292-75124-9 (pbk. : alk. paper)
    1. Nicaragua—Politics and government—1979– 2. Colburn, Forrest D.
I. Title.
F1528.C63 1991
972.8505'3—dc20
                                  90-35718
                                        CIP

Y aparece el Güegüence burlón, picaresco, igualado, desconfiado, haciéndose el sordo y diciendo desde su primera entrada a escena su primera frase de doble sentido.

Pablo Antonio Cuadra
El Nicaragüense

Contents

Preface

FORAYS AS A YOUTH into Mexico from my native San Diego sparked my enduring interest in Latin America and my concern for the region's inequality and generalized poverty. As a graduate student at Cornell, I spent a semester in Guatemala studying rural health paraprofessionals. The stark contrast I encountered between munificence and misery left me with the conviction that the country needed a revolution. So when my mentor proposed I write my dissertation on revolutionary Nicaragua, I eagerly agreed.

I have had many opportunities to observe the richness and complexity of Nicaraguan society. After an eleven-month residence in the country in 1981–1982, I have returned every subsequent year, usually twice, for periods ranging from two weeks to three months to nearly a year (in 1985). Two excursions to Cuba, the first from Nicaragua, heightened my sensitivity to the intricacies of revolution in a small country. Even more enriching were the five months I spent in 1988 teaching at Addis Ababa University, which played a pivotal role in Ethiopia's 1974 Revolution. Ethiopia's intellectuals lost to the army a contest for power, but the University nonetheless provided a window into the country's tumultuous transformation to socialism.

In Nicaragua I have done what I was trained to do—dispassionate scholarship within the *oeuvre* of contemporary "social science." Slowly, though, I realized that, while the mastery of certain kinds of knowledge was facilitated by the methods of scientific inquiry, academic strictures dictated that many facets of everyday life in Nicaragua were not worthy of attention. Or they could only be heeded if they were stripped of their setting, their ambience, to be treated as comparable data.

The impetus to break from my routine and to share diverse personal experiences about revolutionary Nicaragua—to dare to use the first person singular—is threefold. First, there is the poignancy of Nicaragua, so difficult to portray in academic discourse. Second, I have always admired the descriptive accounts of the Mexican Revolution written by such inquisitive intellectuals as Carleton Beals, whose aptly titled *Mexican Maze* was illustrated by Diego Rivera. That genre deserves contemporary emulation.

Most immediately, though, I am inspired by my colleagues in Princeton's history department (I teach in the politics department). Many of them are critical of traditional scholarship for its preoccupation with the elite strata of society—those who govern, those who command, and those who employ. Moreover, only the public lives of the elite are thought to be deserving of study. Traditional history illuminates little of even these people's lives and, worse, tells us nothing about the great majority. History is anonymous.

In retort, and following the lead of French and Italian counterparts, a number of Princeton historians are writing what they call cultural or social history, whose aim is to show how ordinary people live and how they make sense of their lives. In this endeavor to make history more complete, the range of images and experiences judged to be of interest is infinitely broadened. One colleague wrote a book entitled *The Great Cat Massacre and Other Episodes in French Cultural History.* If the Dean let him get away with that, maybe I will not suffer for writing about my car in Managua.

What follows is the piquant transcript etched in my memory of how Nicaragua changed in the first, and undoubtedly most dramatic, decade of post-Somoza rule: what the Sandinistas wrought, and how Nicaraguans interpreted it.

My Car in Managua

BECAUSE THE CHAIRMAN of my dissertation com-
mittee bumped into a former colleague on the Washington subway, I was packed off to Nicaragua in 1981—two
years after the country's celebrated Revolution. I did my
research, had a good time, and went home. But since my
first visit to Nicaragua, I have returned, and returned,
and returned . . . working as a researcher and teacher for
the obscure international mission that sponsored my original visit.

My fourth flight to Managua was to initiate a year's residence. I knew roughly what to expect; however, I found
that six years into the Revolution the capital was more
run-down than it had been two, three, and four years
after the Sandinistas chased Somoza and his cronies off
to Miami. Getting around was much more difficult, too.

Managua was almost completely destroyed by an earthquake in 1972. In the heart of the city, only the country's single skyscraper and the garish, pyramid-shaped
Inter-Continental Hotel survived intact. The fault-
ridden downtown area is off limits, so new construction
is sprawled around its edges. What has emerged is an im-

poverished version of Los Angeles, with transportation just as critical. But by 1985, taxis were rare and buses were becoming more unreliable and unbearably crowded. I had to buy a car.

The first problem was finding one. Local papers carried ads, but none specified an asking price or listed a telephone number. Managua's streets are not named, so addresses are described in relation to the location of a restaurant, a big tree, a burned building, or whatever else catches the eye. From there, one heads off in the direction of—not north, south, east, or west—but the lake, the mountain, up, or down. Even these qualifiers present problems, since Managua is flat and bounded by mountains on three sides. Distance is marked in "blocks," but just what constitutes a block is not agreed upon.

With patience it was possible, in most cases, to locate the address. Then, however, either the car or the owner would not be there. Of course, they would "arrive soon," but I only fell for that line once. I never did manage to find the address, the car, and the owner at the same time.

Someone heard, though, that I—an American—was looking for an inexpensive secondhand car, and soon a Nicaraguan arrived with a 1973 Fiat Berlina. He was unwilling to accept the Nicaraguan currency, the *córdoba.* Instead he wanted four hundred "green parrots," as U.S. dollars are called. At the time there were five exchange rates in Nicaragua: ten, fifteen, twenty-eight, or fifty *córdobas* to the dollar, plus the "legalized black market" rate. When possible, the preference was to dispense with the *córdoba* altogether and *bisnear* in dollars.

I was agreeable to spending $400 for a secondhand

car, but I was not sure about this car. The body was a little saggy, but otherwise presentable, and the upholstery was okay. We took it for a test ride, and the motor held up. Inspecting the car closely, I noticed a few problems, but the owner quickly explained that in Nicaragua my concerns were out of place:

"Only the left windshield wiper works?"

"It is the only one you need."

"The emergency brake doesn't work?"

"You don't need the emergency brake since you leave the car in gear when you park it."

"The signals don't work?"

"Nicaraguans don't use signals."

"The back right door doesn't open?"

"The back left door does."

"The taillights don't work?"

"You only need the front lights to see."

"But can't I get in trouble with the police if I don't have taillights?"

"No, there are no spare light bulbs in the country so the police no longer insist that you have lights."

Once the owner had laid to rest such petty concerns, he launched his sales pitch. Surprisingly, the focus of his harangue was not the motor, the body, or the price—it was the tires. There were no tires to be had in Nicaragua by anyone except government officials. Cars in perfect running condition were parked for lack of tires. This Fiat Berlina, though, had a brand-new set of Bulgarian Vida-VV-Sport tires. He showed them to me, one at a time.

I bought the car.

Registering the car with the revolutionary government

showed just how much civil procedures had changed from the days of Spanish viceroyalties. First, a letter had to be drawn up by a lawyer on legal stationery, bearing an official stamp. It not only described the car but the age, profession, and marital status of the former owner and myself. The letter was signed by the two of us in front of the lawyer and a witness. Then a representative of the institution where I worked wrote out a cover letter stating that I was gainfully employed.

A messenger on a slow motorcycle took the two letters and the former registration card to the Ministry of Foreign Affairs. A week later, the messenger brought back the two letters along with additional letters, informing the Sandinista Police that I had bought a car and asking them to issue a registration card to me. The Institute wrote another cover letter and the messenger on the slow motorcycle returned to "downtown" Managua with all five letters.

Two weeks later he duly announced that the Sandinista Police needed the letter of purchase issued to the previous owner when he bought the car. They also requested the original bill of sale (issued in 1973). Much to my surprise, the former owner produced both documents within a week. The messenger with the slow motorcycle returned to Managua. Two weeks later he showed up again, finally carrying the coveted three-inch-by-five-inch registration card. My name was misspelled beyond recognition, but all the proper forms had been submitted and, I trust, filed.

Finally I was ready to race through the streets of Managua in my Berlina. But then I learned that the requisite tank of gasoline would be a problem. After the Revolution, Mexico and Venezuela agreed to supply Nicaragua with oil on concessionary terms, but Nicaragua never paid a dime to either country, so both had cut off shipments. The Soviets have since assumed responsibility for supplying Nicaragua's oil, but they do not send enough, so gasoline is rationed. (Ironically, the Soviet oil is refined and distributed by Exxon.)

At the beginning of each month every car owner receives coupons for the purchase of twenty gallons of gasoline. With Managua spread out as it is, that amount does not go far. I soon caught on, though, that more can be acquired either by surreptitiously buying extra coupons or by tipping the gas station attendants. Gasoline sold then for 125 *córdobas* a gallon, or 20 cents on the "legalized black market." The going rate for a five-gallon coupon was 200 *córdobas*, while the tip necessary to persuade an attendant to sell you additional gas depends entirely on his perception of how much money you have. My blue eyes and accent entitled me to a special price.

Things get even more difficult when the Soviet tankers are late. Then gas stations open at six or seven in the morning for about half an hour, until their reduced allocation is sold. Lines begin to form as early as 1 A.M. Fights caused by people trying to cut into line break the monotony of waiting. The real excitement, however, comes when an attendant announces at 7 A.M. that he is not going to sell any gas at all that day.

Driving in Managua during the day is relatively straightforward, given the fact that neither turn signals nor brake lights are used. At night it is more dangerous. Many

Nicaraguans use only their high beams for illumination. And you have to watch for people in the street, especially drunks and vendors returning home with their pushcarts. Also, you have to be alert for uncovered manholes, as Managua suffers from a rash of manhole cover thefts.

The missing manhole covers are a great mystery and the subject of much discussion. Why would anyone steal a manhole cover? Perhaps the most compelling explanation of the many proffered is that "manhole covers are stolen by residents of adjoining neighborhoods whose manhole covers were stolen by residents of adjoining neighborhoods whose . . ."

Traffic in Managua is not heavy, but it is varied. There are cars from everywhere: tubby, old American cars and

Willy jeeps, English Land Rovers and squat Hillmans, Renaults and Citroens, Mercedes Benzes and Volkswagens, Volvos, Fiats and Alfa Romeos, Czech Scodas, Soviet Ladas and HHH pickups, and Japanese Mazdas, Toyotas, Datsuns, Mitsubishis, and Isuzu. In the way of trucks, there are old Dodge, Ford, and GMC models, new Soviet Kamazes, and, perhaps most common, East German IFAs, nearly all of which belong to the Sandinista People's Army. The latter are to be reckoned with: they are driven with bravado by young soldiers and their brakes are bad. Indeed, in Managua it is said that IFA stands for *imposible frenar a tiempo* (impossible to stop on time).

There are three kinds of buses: trusty Ford Blue Birds; newer, larger buses that all look the same even though they are variously from Cuba, Spain, Argentina, and Brazil; and small Robur buses from the Soviet Union. Roburs are shaped like a 1950s toaster. Nicaraguans have nicknamed them *roba burro* (rob a burro). Scooters and motorcycles are common, especially East German MZs. The last traffic contingent is the most dangerous: men on horses and oxen or horse-drawn carts (which usually sport automobile tires). None of them "flow with traffic," and none of them have lights.

Surprisingly, this mélange of cars, trucks, buses, motorcycles, horses, and oxen moves relatively smoothly throughout Managua. Traffic lights are abundant and usually work. At major intersections there is normally a policeman with a whistle in his mouth and a fluorescent orange glove on his right hand. He directs traffic. Other policemen, also with orange gloves, are randomly stationed along major arteries. If they catch you committing an infraction, or just want to check your papers, they stop you.

Cars, like my Fiat, that have a license plate identifying the driver as working for an international mission are usually not stopped by the police. But soon after registering my car I was caught crossing a yellow, no-passing line. The orange glove rose defiantly. I halted. The young policeman courteously asked for my driving license. I gave him my U.S. license, which, of course, was in English. He looked at it for the longest time without saying a word or showing a trace of emotion. Then he asked me, "You don't have a driver's license?"

"That's it, brother."

"You may go."

Even though I had escaped the dreaded fine, I thought perhaps I should have a Nicaraguan driver's license. Getting one proved simple since I had the foresight to take to the requisite office a letter of introduction, pictures, and my passport. After only three hours in two offices, I had a license, folded into four pages and inserted in a complimentary plastic case. The front page had a big red star on it. As proud as I was of my new license, friends quickly persuaded me that I would be better treated if I continued using my mystifying U.S. license with the Sandinista police. They suggested that my Sandinista license might "work miracles" with the U.S. police.

Once I became acquainted with the nuances of motoring in Managua, I was free to drive to and from work, and to undertake such projects as combing the city for scarce necessities such as toilet paper and toothpaste.

(Actually, according to the government, there is no shortage of either toilet paper or toothpaste; there is a shortage of the tubes that the former is wrapped around and the latter is contained in.) What I put my Berlina to use for the most, though, was going out in the evenings, especially on weekends.

For those with money, especially dollars, the city has its pleasures. Since dollars can be exchanged for at least twice their official value, foreigners—even young backpackers—can live like the local bourgeoisie whose demise all have come to celebrate. Russians and East Europeans reportedly have also succumbed to the temptation of exchanging dollars on the black market. There is not much to buy in Managua, but a good meal can be found, and the country's rum is beyond compare.

Many visitors check into the Inter-Continental Hotel and, hence, the hotel is the hub of much activity. Howard Hughes once ensconced himself on the top floor (until he was rattled by the 1972 earthquake). Now the hotel caters to rough-and-ready secular missionaries. Revolutionary gossip and rumors are exchanged over rum and Coke in the hotel's bar or across the street at the delightful outdoor cafe, Los Antojitos.

For the most part, Nicaraguan food is plain, especially compared with Mexican and Peruvian dishes. But steaks, seafood, and fruit juices are exceptionally good. The country's premier restaurant is Los Ranchos, which specializes in grilled steaks. The best meal is *puntas de filete a la jalapeña* (fillet of beef with an onion and jalapeño pepper cream sauce).

The Lobster Inn offers fresh red snapper, shrimp, and

lobster. The tantalizing mixed-seafood cocktail is named "Return to Life." The ambience is enhanced by a small pool containing turtles and two small alligators. The surrounding fence was raised after a careless Libyan learned just how quickly alligators snap their jaws.

For adventure, there is the Walpa Tara, a small restaurant offering Miskito Indian food, including turtle, rabbit, and armadillo. The armadillo stew is especially good. I soon learned that only the foolhardy sample Managua's street food, which can be more appetizing than the fare in most restaurants, but carries the risk of illness. (Most street vendors are well meaning, but there was a distressing incident reported in the newspapers in which someone's "chicken" proved to be buzzard.)

After a hearty meal, one can go dancing. The "in" discotheque never changes—it has always been Lobo Jack (*lobo* means wolf, the name thus being a takeoff on the American radio personality Wolfman Jack). Lobo Jack used to be the private discotheque of Somoza's National Guard. With the Revolution it was nationalized, and is now a state enterprise, part of the economic vanguard of the Revolution. On any weekend evening, Lobo Jack's dance floor is packed with Nicaraguans letting loose, not to Cuban salsa, but to the music of Michael Jackson and other *gringos*. Foreign patrons add a bit of character— and seediness. For a while there was heady competition between the Libyans who offered pretty girls U.S. $100 bills, and Marines from the U.S. Embassy, who made vague promises of visas to *gringolandia*.

Also there are the movies: Managua has more than a dozen movie theaters, offering a selection of movies to be found nowhere else. There are raunchy Mexican movies, Argentine soft-porn flicks, Kung Fu movies from wherever they come from, vintage Italian and French movies, American movies that were box office duds in the "colossus of the north" (with titles like *Girls in Sweaters* and *Human Experiment*), Cuban homages to the Cuban Revolution, and movies from the Soviet Union and Eastern Europe.

Most Nicaraguans prefer Mexican movies, while what is left of the middle and upper classes prefers sleek American ones, with James Bond's *Octopussy* heading the list. After one Mexican movie you understand why Nicaraguans say, "There are good movies, there are bad movies, and there are Mexican movies."

Anytime you go out for a meal, dancing, or a movie you encounter the "car watchers." As you get out of the car you are approached by someone—often a child—who asks if you want your car watched. You must say yes, otherwise you have no idea what will happen to it while you are away. When you return, someone will charge you for watching your car. Often this is not the same person whom you agreed to have watch your car, but it does not matter. Anyone getting into a car in Managua can be charged a small fee by anyone else.

Actually, a good car watcher is worth the price. With the dire economic situation in Managua there has been a rash of thefts of car parts from unguarded parked cars. My rearview mirror disappeared one night. I was spared more serious losses thanks to one of the problems with my car: the latch for the hood was broken. To raise the hood it was necessary to reach under the left fender and pull a special wire that had been rigged up to serve as a latch.

Another difficulty with having a car in Managua is deciding how to handle the hordes of hitchhikers. Each year since the Revolution, fewer and fewer buses serve the city. Consequently, those without cars have audaciously adopted the American custom of hitchhiking. Even solitary, elderly women stick out their thumbs. Any driver who stops at an intersection is likely to be subjected to desperate pleas for a "ride," the English word Nicaraguans use but which they spell "raid."

My trusty Fiat ferried many a Nicaraguan from one part of the city to another. It is hard to drive past people who have waited an hour for a bus that may not ever come. Besides, Nicaraguans always have something to say. Those over twenty-five talked mostly about the economic crisis. Girls and young women flattered me by asking if I was married or if I had a girlfriend. Young men out of uniform talked mostly about Nicaragua's obligatory military service: some dreaded it, while others could not wait to be called up. Among the latter, the ultimate status symbol was to show up at a party with an AK-47. Soldiers who climbed in and out of my tiny car with their packs and automatic rifles seemed much more sober, suggesting that they knew what the ubiquitous AK-47s were really for.

It did not take long to master the idiosyncrasies of my car and of driving in Managua. But no sooner did I get the feel of it than the battery gave out. Batteries are scarce in Managua, so for two months I had to look for people to push my car wherever I went. But Nicaraguans

are out in the street a lot; they do not stay cooped-up in their houses. There is always someone around to push-start a stalled car.

One hot Saturday, I decided to find a battery. I went from one grimy repair shop to another. Everywhere the answer was the same: "There are no batteries." Finally, out of desperation, I told a mechanic who had assured me there were no batteries to be bought in all of Managua, "I will pay you in dollars." Without blinking an eye he said, "Come by at eight tomorrow morning and I'll have one for you." A $20 bill put an end to the great shortage.

The progressive disintegration of my muffler threatened to send me back to Managua's repair shops. But in my search for a battery I had never seen anyone working on mufflers. And since in all of Nicaragua there are only five elevators and one escalator (which does not work), I could not believe I would find a garage with a hydraulic lift. Yet, without free access to the underneath of the car, how could a mechanic replace a rusted muffler?

Just as elsewhere, muffler work in Nicaragua is done by a specialist. I followed the oblique directions I was given to the "best place in Managua." Instead of a hydraulic lift there was a deep trench dug out of the soft earth. I nervously pulled my car over one end of the trench. The mechanic jumped into the other end of the hole and went to work with a bunch of pipes and a welding torch. His chickens and roosters cooperated by staying away from the torch's flame.

A more serious problem arose when I hit one pothole too many. One of the axle braces broke, and the right front wheel nearly fell off. An ensuing tour of Nicaragua's wrecking yards convinced me that this was the best business in the country, but that the brace I needed was nowhere to be found. A welder was coaxed to do what all claimed was impossible—repair the broken brace— but only after I persuaded him I was not one of the "communist internationalists" who had made it impossible for him to live as well as he had before the Revolution. The mechanic who put the car back together lost a couple of bolts, but after he disappeared under the car with a coat hanger and a wire cutter, he proclaimed that the bolts were no longer necessary.

In time, I came to feel very affectionately toward my Berlina, which my friends had jokingly nicknamed the *balazo* (the shot). It was slow and it made me aware of every pothole I crossed, but it became familiar to me in a country where everything was unfamiliar. Like almost everyone, I am susceptible to loving the familiar. Also, my Fiat unwittingly came to serve as an uncontested letter of introduction to the nuances of the Nicaraguan Revolution. And for that I am most grateful.

Hermes Baby

OFF TO THE SIDE of the sprawling Roberto Huembes market is a small museum, the Museum of the Revolution. The Museum has a sign, but its existence is made more apparent by the three tanks and an enormous piece of twisted bronze, torn from a statue, that together adorn the entrance to the Museum. One tiny two-barreled tank, about the size of my Fiat, was a gift from Mussolini to Somoza. Another tank was captured from Somoza's National Guard by the Sandinistas. The third tank, Sandinista from its christening, is homemade and looks it. When the Sandinistas triumphed, a jubilant mob pulled down the statue of Somoza which stood in front of the National Stadium (itself in ruins from the 1972 earthquake). The fragment on display in front of the Museum of the Revolution is all that is left of the Big Man on Horseback: half of a horse's ass.

Inside the building, the contemporary history of Nicaragua is traced through the personal effects and photos of its principal actors. U.S. Marines occupied Nicaragua almost continuously from 1909 until 1933. Interventions were ostensibly motivated by a variety of concerns; there was talk of stability and democracy, and obscure references to the Panama Canal and debts to New York banks. In the end, the Marines stayed just to battle a guerrilla army led by Augusto Sandino, whose sole purpose, in turn, was to oust the Yankees. The Museum has lots of pictures of U.S. Marines marching, riding burros, standing in front of a bullet-riddled fort, and flying the U.S. flag. There is a picture of a downed Fokker plane that was vainly used to bomb Sandino and his soldiers. Finally, there is a picture of a black Ford truck carrying the mortal remains of an unlucky Marine.

There are many pictures of Sandino and his troops, as well. Sandino was a small man who wore a big hat and tucked his trousers into high, laced boots. In one display case there is the leather jacket Sandino wore on his 1930 trip to Mexico. Ironically, it was kept safely in San Francisco until 1979.

The U.S. Marines withdrew without ever having caught Sandino. In their place they left a hastily trained National Guard. Anastasio Somoza soon emerged as its leader. He invited Sandino to come down out of the hills and talk peace. Sandino came down and was murdered. In 1936, Somoza overthrew the elected president, paving the way for his family dynasty.

The Museum of the Revolution has a number of Somoza's personal effects. It gets confusing, though, because there were three Somozas. Anastasio Somoza had two sons, Luis and Anastasio Junior. When the old man was assassinated in 1956 (by a poet), Luis took over. When Luis died of a heart attack in 1967, Junior became head of state. Nicaraguans are not always clear about which Somoza they are referring to when discussing Nicaragua's history. Maybe it does not matter. Anyway, in the Museum there is Luis's Smith and Wesson .38 Special. There is a Harvard University identification card issued to Anastasio Somoza, and a similar card from the Harvard Cooperative Society, listing Anastasio as a permanent member. There is Somoza's license plate, featuring five red stars and the bald statement, "President of the Republic." An entire display cabinet is given over to the medals Somoza presented to himself. I got dizzy counting them, but ended—accurately or not—with 196. There are pictures too: Somoza with the local Catholic hierarchy, Somoza giving candy at Christmas to children of members of the National Guard, Somoza with Franklin Roosevelt, Somoza with Richard Nixon, and Somoza with John Kennedy. Somoza is always smiling.

Most of the Museum is devoted to the guerrillas who took on—and defeated—the Somozas. There are large, blown-up photos of the nine men who, in 1961, organized themselves into a cabal, the Front for Sandinista National Liberation (FSLN). They named themselves Sandinistas in homage to Sandino. Of the nine, only one, Tomás Borge, has survived. In display cases are the personal effects of the nine and of subsequent recruits. There is a Hermes Baby typewriter used to bang out pronouncements and proclamations. There is the Boy Scout uniform of one cherished martyr.

And there are more pictures. In one a captured Daniel Ortega is led to prison (where he wrote a poem titled, "I never saw Managua when miniskirts were in fashion"). Recognizing the surviving Sandinistas is difficult, not so much because they have aged, but because their faces used to be obscured by long hair, sideburns, moustaches, and beards. All the hair, and the style in which it is brandished, attest to the awareness among Nicaraguan youth in the 1960s and 1970s of what their peers were up to in places as distant as Berkeley and Paris.

Outnumbering everything else in the Museum, though, are pistols, rifles, pipe bombs, machine guns, and mortars. It is not clear if the pipe bombs are replicas. In one gruesome exhibit there is a stained shirt with a prominent hole. Next to the shirt, fitted over a mannequin, is a suspended automatic rifle with a hole in the magazine clip. A bullet of the National Guard pierced the clip and continued into the chest of the Sandinista *comandante*, Germán Pomares.

The Museum reminds you that the course of politics is decided by individuals and the choices they make. But as you step out of the poorly attended Museum, the panorama of Nicaraguans hawking goods and clambering aboard old buses seems distant from the country's political struggles of the last few decades.

McDonald's

AMONG THE CENTRAL AMERICAN jet set, the quality ranking of Big Macs in the region is: Panama, Guatemala, El Salvador, Costa Rica, and, at the bottom, Nicaragua. (Honduras's McDonald's was shut down long ago by McDonald's International for repeated quality violations.) Problems in Nicaragua since the Revolution have made it impossible for Managua's McDonald's to maintain the Golden Arches' standards. I know the son of the owner of McDonald's Managua and he regularly kept me abreast of the lack of sympathy from McDonald's International. Trouble with the "parent company" began with a stern letter warning McDonald's Managua, among other things, that it is "not to sell cheeseburgers unless they contain cheese."

McDonald's Managua, established in 1975, was cleverly placed in the middle of a shopping center dominated by a large movie theater, a bowling alley, and the Lobo Jack discotheque. McDonald's Managua's business has always been good, but the 1979 Revolution brought many changes. Customers, for example, often entered carrying assorted automatic assault rifles and machine guns. But the owner of Managua's McDonald's never had anything to do with Somoza, so the business was not confiscated when the Sandinistas seized power.

However, the Sandinistas' bid to transform Nicaragua, and the counterrevolution it engendered, have occasioned a host of difficulties for McDonald's Managua. Obtaining supplies has become problematic. Nicaragua's scarcity of foreign exchange put an end to such imports as pickles and "official" Big Mac wrapping paper. But even obtaining locally produced goods such as bread, meat, cheese, potatoes, and lettuce is a continuous headache. Keeping McDonald's well lit is a problem too—there are shortages of light bulbs in the new Nicaragua. Finally, maintaining a cadre of young, energetic, and cheerful employees has been hampered by the "Popular Sandinista Army's" recruitment. Employee termination is sometimes announced only by the arrival of an IFA army truck in front of the Golden Arches.

McDonald's Managua has responded to the difficulties with creativity and good humor. As one of McDonald's managers explained, "When we don't have yellow cheese, we use white cheese. When we don't have lettuce, we use cabbage. And when we don't have french fries, we sell deep-fried cassava." Of course, there are occasional stopgap measures that do not work. For a while McDonald's tried using Russian wrapping paper for its Big Macs. But by the time customers walked to their tables, the paper gave the Big Macs the odor of "wet cardboard." The managers of McDonald's Managua astutely quit using the wrapping paper.

While McDonald's Managua fed hungry Nicaraguans

at a modest price, word filtered back to McDonald's International that the Managua outpost was selling substandard Big Macs and that sometimes, instead of regulation Coca-Cola, the beverage of the day was *pitaya* (a tropical cactus fruit drink). McDonald's International received such disturbing news not from flabbergasted American tourists, but from American journalists who delighted in including detailed accounts of Managua's Big Macs in their dispatches. McDonald's International worried about its image, an image that aims to persuade loyal customers that anywhere in the world they see the Golden Arches they can count on exactly the same hamburger, french fries, and soft drink they enjoy back home.

McDonald's International might also have been worried about its money. McDonald's Managua was supposed to pay royalties, and, in fact, the owner regularly deposited the stipulated percentage of revenues in a bank account. The problem is that since the Sandinistas came to power they have not provided foreign exchange, which they control, for the reparation of profits. They have, however, increased the money supply, resulting in *de facto* devaluations of the *córdoba*. At the onset of Sandinista rule the dollar was worth 10 *córdobas*. The black market steadily devalued the *córdoba* to an ever-diminishing fraction of its value. Indeed, every $1,000 McDonald's International had in Managua in late 1979 was worth less than $5 by 1985. And McDonald's International could not even have its $5.

For all the billions of hamburgers McDonald's has sold worldwide, it was powerless to discipline its Nicaraguan brethren. McDonald's International wrote a series of polite but forceful letters. The only concession McDonald's International offered was that "McDonald's Managua may sell Big Macs without pickles." Other than writing letters, there was not much McDonald's International could do. It could have attempted to dismantle the Golden Arches in Managua by filing a legal suit in Nicaragua. But that measure would have been time-consuming, expensive, and probably unsuccessful. Even if they did get an injunction, who would enforce it? The Sandinista Police?

Finally, my friend's father took pity on the tormented executives of McDonald's International and, in early 1988, voluntarily changed the name of his contentious business from McDonald's to Donald's. McDonald's International was satisfied just to be symbolically cut loose from its Managua renegade. By that time the black market had reduced its royalties to pennies, which were still uncollectible anyway. As for the Managua branch losing its heralded name, a manager explained: "We sell our hamburgers because they are the best in Managua, not because of our name." The retort is credible. Sandy's—a fast-food competitor—sometimes sells meatless hamburgers.

The Bulgarians

GEORGE BALL ONCE COMPLAINED that while he was the U.S. undersecretary of state, a monthly call in the middle of the night would awaken him telling of a coup in some distant capital with a name like a typographical error. "Managua, Nicaragua" could have dazed Ball at 2 A.M. Since Ball's era, though, the Sandinistas have made Managua a household word. Everyone except the rich and the completely unadventurous is visiting the city—for a fact-finding tour, advice, a pilgrimage; to give away someone else's money; to report, spy, scold, show sympathy or solidarity. Some people come just for a look around. There are throngs of idle young from everywhere. Distinguished visitors range from the Pope and the late Maurice Bishop to Allen Ginsberg and the head of the Italian Communist party. Even the defense minister of the People's Democratic Republic of Yemen, Brigadier General Saleh Mosleh Kassem, has stopped by for consultations. Iran has established an embassy, as has Mongolia (though the Mongolian ambassador is "not in residence"). There are constant visits from Castro's messengers. The CIA and KGB are presumably in town.

Efforts are being made to further bolster the throngs of visitors. The Nicaraguan government has decided tourism is not so bad. Rather tired-looking brochures have been printed up, emphasizing Nicaragua's natural beauty and historical sites. The brochures make no mention of the country's revolution or counterrevolution. They could have been printed in the 1950s. But to date, it does not appear that Nicaragua has been able to attract the camera-toting, Bermuda-shorts-wearing big spenders. There are only the political pilgrims.

The focus of attention on Nicaragua and the resultant horde of visitors are pressed into helping resolve the local shortage of dollars. Before visitors even get to the airport immigration booths (patterned after those in Havana), they are required to exchange $60 at the official government rate, which fails to cover cab fare to the city. Foreign governments and international organizations have provided generous support, which has actually increased since President Reagan stopped U.S. aid. The annual value of foreign assistance exceeds the value of exports by a hefty margin. The varying guises of such assistance—and the accompanying technicians—add to Managua's charm. For example, so many countries have donated ambulances that no two seem to have the same siren.

The most noticed and commented-upon foreign presence in Nicaragua has not been Cuban, Soviet, Mexican, or Venezuelan, but Bulgarian. The Bulgarians have seemingly put their fingers in everything. Statistics on the total number of Bulgarians in Nicaragua and their activities have not been divulged, but announcements of

Bulgaria's participation in various types of projects are common. For example, Bulgaria is helping to build a deepwater port on the Caribbean coast that supposedly will be the largest in Central America. Bulgaria is also involved in the development of copper, lead, and zinc mines in the interior of the country. Even a local basketball coach reported getting tips from a Bulgarian "sports specialist."

The Nicaraguan government has purchased everything from machinery for a ketchup factory to a watercooled computer mainframe from Bulgaria. There is also a wide variety of Bulgarian consumer goods in Nicaraguan markets. Perla, a common brand of toothpaste in the country, is Bulgarian.

Surprisingly, with the fanfare appropriate for celebrating a major shift in Nicaraguan popular culture, the independent Nicaraguan newspaper, La Prensa, reported on the arrival of a new baby food, "Bulgarian Gerbers." (Gerber Products Co., of Fremont, Michigan, provided virtually all baby food in Nicaragua, via their Costa Rican distributor, until it became impossible to obtain payment in dollars for their mushed peas. Nicaraguans now use "Gerber" as a generic name for baby food, and Gerber Products, U.S.A., says these Gerbers have no connection with their baby food.)

Recent economic difficulties in Nicaragua have led to periodic shortages of such staples as corn, bread, milk, meat, and cooking oil. However, state-run supermarkets are full of Bulgarian canned peaches and fruit preserves (strawberry, raspberry, plum, cherry, and fig). Why does a Central American country that produces an abundance

of tropical fruit and is in dire financial shape spend scarce foreign exchange on Bulgarian canned peaches?

Bulgaria's incentive is partially monetary. Trade between the two countries is at roughly $65 million. Rumors in Managua suggest, with some validity, that socialist countries have quietly urged Nicaragua to retain its traditional Western export markets, but to switch its import markets to socialist countries, which are pressed for hard foreign exchange. Bulgaria may be capitalizing on the Nicaraguan market to unload unmarketable merchandise. Where else, for example, can Bulgaria sell its Gerbers (which, according to a Gerber Products, U.S.A., spokesman, "taste terrible")? Bulgaria also earns foreign exchange by having at least some of its advisers paid in dollars and by providing such services as the foreign marketing of Nicaragua's tobacco. Bulgaria has offered extensive credit on lenient terms and provided some donations. True, credit has been earmarked for the purchase of Bulgarian goods, and donations have been in kind, not in cash, but assistance has been at levels high enough to suggest that more than a profit motive underlies Bulgaria's presence in Nicaragua. The Nicaraguan government claims that Bulgarian assistance is yet another example of socialist solidarity. Numerous Bulgarian jokes making the rounds in Nicaragua are more skeptical. One example: after working for some time in Nicaragua, a Bulgarian adviser began to yearn for the food of his native country. He went from restaurant to restaurant asking for goulash, only to receive the same reply: "We have chicken, pork, beef, fish, shrimp, and lobster, but no goulash." When he returned home, his boss asked about his impressions of Nicaragua. "Very backward," the adviser said. "They eat like we ate twenty years ago."

Turtle Eggs and
Turbö Tennis Shoes

LIKE EVERYWHERE ELSE, shopping in Nicaragua is a prosaic chore. But the Revolution has made it decidedly less mundane.

There are numerous places to buy—or at least look for—what you need. There are supermarkets, sprawling outdoor markets, one shopping mall, "mom and pop, sister and brother" general stores, neighbors, employers, neighborhood Sandinista Defense Committees, and, since 1984, a swank store that accepts only dollars, the Diplo. Some Nicaraguans have decided preferences for which of the above they patronize. Others, particularly those in isolated rural areas, necessarily have their options narrowed. But many Nicaraguans show up everywhere, largely because you never know what you will—or will not—find in any given locale. There are plenty of surprises.

The government intermittently offers some basic foodstuffs through neighborhood defense committees. Quantities are limited, but prices are low. Also, government bureaucracies and enterprises sometimes offer something for nothing, or next to nothing. Workers at the huge Chiltepe dairy farm, for example, get a free liter of milk daily.

There are understandable limits to government largess, so forays must be made. Initially, Nicaragua's supermarkets were favorites, and indeed overwhelmed by throngs. The nationalization of the country's largest supermarkets made them an ideal instrument for the government "to help the people with people's prices." Shelves were stripped bare, not only to fill cupboards, but also for resale elsewhere. Concomitantly, for a number of reasons, the local production of consumer goods and foodstuffs began to decline. A prominent problem, recognized only later, was that price controls intended to aid consumers weakened farmers' incentives.

Relatively quickly, supermarkets became rather curious places. They are usually bereft of necessities. There will be no milk, eggs, rice, beans, meat, or bread. Instead, the supermarkets are stocked with strange assortments of merchandise. Cleaning supplies are abundant: soap, brushes, brooms, mops, and rakes. Condiments are available, including sometimes four different brands of vinegar. Odd products show up, such as plastic car seat cushions.

What the supermarkets really excel in, though, is imported goods, which appear and disappear. For a time there were tins of tasty Soviet sardines. But there were also cans of strange meats and sausages from somewhere in Eastern Europe. These cans remained on the shelves until the bourgeoisie discovered they made excellent pet food. Other goods that have intermittently appeared on the shelves range from Cuban rum to Canadian hamburger relish, to Italian jam, to Chinese chocolate bars. At any one time, however, supermarkets never really have enough of everything. So one product will be spread out over a whole aisle, one deep on the wide shelves.

Nicaraguan supermarkets also sell cosmetics, books, stationery, clothes, and pots and pans. No attempt is made to be comprehensive. Whatever is available is put out for sale. The diversity is stunning. Pond's Cold Cream stands next to unidentifiable Bulgarian cosmetics. There are posters of Santa Claus and books from Moscow's Progress Publishers with such titles as *Comunismo Científico*. There may be no cheese in the store, but there will be an aisle's worth of cheese graters.

The shortcomings of Nicaragua's supermarkets have prompted shoppers to rely more heavily on Nicaragua's traditional markets, where legions of vendors offer their goods. Every town and city has its market. Some merchants have stalls; others only have a basket full of whatever they have to sell. Anyone can enter the market and sell anything anyone will buy. The attitude towards competition is shrug-of-the-shoulder generosity: as one woman told me, "Everyone has to eat."

Managua has three large markets named after Sandinista martyrs. The fourth, and by far the largest, market is still known as the Mercado Oriental (the Eastern Market). It is enormous, covering dozens of square blocks and employing thousands. Here you can find everything, even, I was once told, "a nuclear-powered helicopter." Vehicles can worm their way through the periphery of

the market, deeper only with difficulty, and in the center
it is impossible. Either side of the street can be six deep
with vendors. Someone may have a bucket of turtle eggs,
another a rickety table covered with radios, the third an
old sewing machine. Next may be a child with three
hand towels, a woman with a glowing barbecue and
crackling pork skin, and finally there is a store, the business of which is often obfuscated by all the commotion
outside.

Just where goods in the Mercado Oriental come from
is a mystery. One can, for example, find brands of tennis
shoes unknown elsewhere: Amerika, Jaguar, Kidocs, and

Turbö. Some goods are reportedly stolen from poorly guarded government warehouses. Others are brought into Nicaragua by petty traders willing to put up with the ex-actions of customs authorities. Foodstuffs, of course, are trucked in from the countryside.

Clothes and sundry goods can also be purchased at Nicaragua's sole shopping mall—the Commercial Center Managua. Here crowds are less crushing, but prices are higher. One shops in stores with discrete names: the Hope Store sells plastic pails, the Chance Store sells radios, the Syrian Store sells baby clothes, and IMELSA sells magazines and books from Nicaragua, Vietnam, Cuba, and the Soviet Union. From the latter you can buy the magazine *STP* (which stands for *Socialismo, Teoría y Práctica*), and leaf through it while you enjoy coconut ice cream at Pops.

The aging Commercial Center has been displaced from its shopping zenith by the Diplo. For payment in dollars, the Diplo offers what cannot be found even in the inner recesses of the Mercado Oriental: Whirlpool refrigerators, Hoover vacuum cleaners, Mother Goose coloring books, Christian Dior perfume, Old El Paso Hot Taco Sauce, and Fab Full Strength Detergent. The only product from Nicaragua is coffee; the only good from the Soviet Union is Stolichnaya Vodka. Although the Diplo is an abbreviation of Diplomat, the government-owned and operated store is open to anyone whose wallet is full of dollars.

Most Nicaraguans, though, do not have dollars, or even much in the way of *córdobas*, and most live far from Managua. Aside from their own labors and the local open-air market, these disenfranchised Nicaraguans look to small, family-run general stores. Yet most of these cannot be counted on having much more than rum, rotting plantains, and stale crackers. The paucity of goods gives credence to the rural adage, "Many are the Indians, few are the tamales."

Neighbors often have something to trade, though—onions perhaps, tortillas, or maybe mangos. Here sellers and buyers are cut from the same cloth. Their intertwining commerce serves as a reminder that trading is also a means of scraping together a living. One hand feeds the other.

Reading the Newspapers

MANAGUA IS NOT A CITADEL of the belles lettres or scientific inquiry. An old joke about the city, one that antedates the Revolution, asks, "What two things can you leave in an unlocked car without worry of theft?" The answer: "A book and a necktie." But with the Revolution, and the ensuing politicization of city and country life, Managua's newspapers are as spirited and engaging as any found elsewhere. Every day, the city's three newspapers hit the streets with headlines of a size befitting the beginning and ending of world war.

The three contentious newspapers are each under the editorship of a member of the Chamorro family, symbolizing perhaps that the Revolution is a division within the Nicaraguan family. *La Prensa* is the opposition newspaper. It was in opposition to Somoza; it is in opposition to the Sandinistas. *El Nuevo Diario* is a private newspaper as well, but it is committed to the Revolution and Sandinista leadership. It was established by a Chamorro formerly with *La Prensa* who was angered by the newspaper's lack of sympathy for the Revolution. *Barricada* is the *Organo Oficial del Frente Sandinista de Liberación Na-*

cional. Ironically, *Barricada* is published with the same printing facilities that once spewed out Somoza's broadsheet, *Novedades.*

In the other countries of Central America, newspapers are devoted largely to the reporting of international news and local traffic accidents, either because it is too dangerous to report on national issues (witness Guatemala) or because there is just not that much to say about the polity (as in Honduras). In Nicaragua, though, everything is a big deal—or at least an attempt is made to make it a big deal. Nicaraguans avidly read their newspapers. But they do not read them to find out what has happened, or what is going to happen. Naked information is gleaned from rumors, which spread unbelievably fast, perhaps because of the prevalence of large families and Nicaraguans' penchant for gab. Newspapers are read to see the puffy reactions, the official and that of the opposition, to events. Revealingly, sometimes front-page news is simply a commentary on (usually a denial of) a rumor sweeping through Managua.

The censure and periodic closing of *La Prensa* by the Sandinistas have made it the most widely known newspaper in Latin America. *La Prensa* represents the right to dissent. The mast of the newspaper proclaims, "Without freedom of the press there is no freedom." But *La Prensa*, when published, is not particularly enlightened. In its relentless effort to discredit the Sandinista regime, it is one-sided, negative, ideological, and even sensational. A characteristic headline reads: "National Demand: New Government." An illuminating joke about the newspaper: one of the nine *comandantes* who comprise the ruling Sandinista National Directorate, Tomás Borge, announces he is going to make his first visit *ever* to the sea. Off he goes, followed by an entourage of national and international reporters. Arriving at the beach, Borge disrobes and strolls down to the water. To the amazement of everyone, he walks on the water. The stunned journalists begin scribbling furiously. The next day *La Prensa* announces: "Borge Can't Swim!"

La Prensa is worth reading for its sarcastic criticism of the Sandinistas, Fidel, the Soviet Union, and scientific socialism. Once, for example, it published two pages of pictures showing Afghan guerrillas atop destroyed Soviet tanks. The captions were borrowed from Sandinista phraseology, proclaiming, for example: "A heroic people, united in the struggle to smash imperialism."

El Nuevo Diario is the least interesting of Nicaragua's newspapers. It combines the staid revolutionary line with a dash of sensationalism, provided in the form of traffic accident photos and narratives of heinous crimes.

Barricada offers the greatest insight into the Nicaraguan Revolution, and is the best-crafted of the newspapers. It always has a calculated sense of urgency, even when the headline is "The Toys Have Arrived!" (The November 24, 1988, issue announced the arrival of Cuban, Bulgarian, and Soviet toys, a shipment which included Multy dolls for girls and plastic pistols for boys.) More commonly, the machinations of the United States are denounced; revolutionary decrees are announced; distinguished visitors, like the Vietnamese General Giap, are shown receiving their Order of Sandino; Nicaraguans are exhorted to heed the draft, plant corn and beans, pick coffee, save electricity and water, report speculators, denounce counterrevolutionaries, and curb their demands on their hard-pressed government.

Politics recedes at the back of the newspaper, where one finds such articles as "Fax Fever in Washington," "The World of Stevie Wonder," and "Black Is the Most Popular Color" (in West German fashion). Television listings are provided for the Sandinista Television System. Regular programs include "Sandinista News," "Scooby Doo," "Boney," and "Flipper." Also, there are advertisements, for example, Yard-Man lawnmowers at Motorama.

But what really dominates the back pages of Barricada, and El Nuevo Diario and La Prensa as well, is baseball.

Nicaraguans have been *fanáticos* for baseball since 1909, when the sport was introduced by U.S. Marines. Notwithstanding testy relations with the United States, *Barricada* reports on the fortunes of U.S. major league teams.

In fact, many Nicaraguans have a favorite major league team. (It is considered politically incorrect, though, for your favored team to be *los Yanquis*.) Of course, local teams receive the most coverage. But a U.S. Marine could understand the stories—so much of the vocabulary is English:

hits	strike	shortstop
no hitter	out	manager
club	right field	inning
lineup	bullpen	clutch
home plate	staff	double play

Other words differ only in their spelling; for example, homerun is spelled *jonrón*. Interest in, and newspaper coverage of, baseball seems to be inversely related to politics. The less screaming about politics, the more yelling about baseball.

My favorite part of *Barricada* is the political comics of Nicaragua's celebrated cartoonist, Róger Sánchez Flores. All Nicaraguans—even those in opposition to the government—enjoy his cartoons. And they have been reproduced in English, Russian, German, Swedish, and Italian. He has won a number of international prizes, including a West German competition featuring the work of cartoonists from more than thirty countries.

Róger, as he signs his work, has never had any formal training in art. His first noteworthy cartoon was of a professor sketched on the back of an exam; he failed the exam. He began drawing cartoons for *La Prensa*, but after the Revolution he joined the staff of *Barricada*.

The cartoons mimic a pantheon of characters—speculators, the bourgeoisie, government bureaucrats, the *contra* (Nicaraguan counterrevolutionaries), the CIA, and the Reagan and Bush administrations. Each of his caricatures has become familiar to Nicaraguans: speculators are portrayed as crocodiles, the bourgeoisie as middle-aged men in suits and top hats, the *contra* as Somoza's National Guard (GN), the CIA as spindly spooks in dark glasses and trench coats. Uncle Sam is Uncle Sam.

One memorable cartoon that poked fun at the "colossus to the north" showed a rocket approaching the moon. In the second caption the rocket, identified as USA, has landed and soldiers exit. In the final caption

an officer proclaims, "Remember, we are here to defend the national security of the United States."

In an assault on the bourgeoisie, a dumpy lawyer is shown reading a will to a bereaved woman and her cigar-smoking son. Behind them stands their chauffeur, humbly holding his hat. The lawyer reads, "Being of sound mind, I leave half of my factories to my wife and the other half to my son. I irrevocably will my entire ideology to Juan, my chauffeur."

As years have passed, though, Róger has increasingly caricatured bureaucrats. One cartoon shows a Nicaraguan saying to a seated bureaucrat, ". . . and that is my problem, can you help me?" The bureaucrat replies, "No, not at all." The dialogue is twice repeated between two other Nicaraguans and the slovenly bureaucrat. In the final caption the bureaucrat's supervisor arrives and asks, "Any trouble with your work?" The still seated bureaucrat replies, "No, not at all."

Taken together, *La Prensa*, *El Nuevo Diario*, and *Barricada* provide a multifaceted transcript of Nicaraguan society. Differences in their interpretations of personages and events are real but an important similarity among the three dailies can be seen. As a peasant once remarked to me, "Since the Revolution, all the newspapers in Nicaragua have more pictures of people who look like me." Gone, even from *La Prensa*, are photos of debutantes, engagements, weddings, cocktail parties, embassy receptions, and balls.

Driving outside Managua

AS I GAINED CONFIDENCE in my car, I ventured farther and farther out of Managua. While there is little beauty within Managua, the surrounding countryside is gorgeous. The city borders on a large lake, Lake Managua (unfortunately so polluted that it is held by biologists to be dead). Within view are two volcanos, Momotombo, and beside it, little Momotombo, called Momotombito by Nicaraguans. From May to December there is lush vegetation bathed by warm rains (what Nicaraguans, without shame, call winter). During the rest of the year, the vegetation wilts because there is little rain (this they call summer).

A favorite outing of residents of Managua is to head off in the direction of Momotombo towards Xiloá, a peaceful lagoon situated in a volcanic crater. It is half an hour's drive for a swim in Xiloá's tranquil waters. The lagoon used to have no public facilities. Anyone could come for a picnic and a swim, but unless you had a private home there, as many wealthy Nicaraguans did, you made do with what nature offered. With the Revolution, public facilities were installed, with some creativity and taste. And despite Nicaragua's precipitous economic decline, there are always Nicaraguans relaxing at Xiloá. I have never decided whether the persistent crowds meant that some people always have money no matter what is happening, or simply that no matter what is going on people will go for a swim.

There are a couple of military bases near the lagoon. One Saturday, in an isolated corner of the lagoon, I came upon two off-duty soldiers who were fishing with a grenade. They threw the grenade in the water, and after it exploded, they swam around collecting the stunned fish that floated to the surface. They had a couple of dozen fish, enough they claimed for a "rich" soup. By their account, with things the way they were, it was hard to get a good meal, and one had to be resourceful.

A longer drive, this one to the west, would take friends and me to the beaches of the Pacific. Pochomil, the closest beach, takes an hour, while others—including some completely isolated ones—a bit longer. Nicaragua's coastline is beautiful and unspoiled. The only intrusions are welcome—an occasional rickety restaurant with *música romántica*, offering grilled red snapper, fried plantain, and rice. There is cold beer and rum. If you do not drink alcohol, as I do not, you ask for a rum with Coke on the side. Drink the Coke and leave the rum as a tip. There is a shortage of Coke in Nicaragua, so restaurants only sell Coke with the more expensive rum.

Alternative excursions from Managua are to such nearby cities as Masaya and Granada. There is not much in Masaya itself, but just outside the city is an active volcano, Santiago, billowing smoke. You can drive right to the edge of the crater. If the wind is just right—it almost never is—you can see the red glow of molten lava. Somoza's National Guard is rumored to have dropped political prisoners into the crater from a helicopter. Between the volcano and Masaya is the Masaya Lagoon, set deep in a volcanic crater.

Granada is situated on the edge of Lake Nicaragua, which is famous for its freshwater sharks. The sharks, dangerous as any, supposedly exist because an eon ago the lake was part of the sea. Granada is more endearing than Managua, and not only because earthquakes are always leveling Managua. Historically, there were two important cities in Nicaragua, Granada and León. Granada was dominated by conservatives, León by liberals. They hated each other and fought ruinous battles. Peace came only when they settled their rivalry by choosing Managua, then a sleepy town, as Nicaragua's capital.

No one from Granada ever told me how León was founded. But a colleague from León gleefully explained to me how Granada was settled. A Spanish sloop carrying three hundred whores to Lima was battered and blown off course by a ferocious storm. The ship sailed up the San Juan River into Lake Nicaragua and across it to the shore of what is now Granada.

Granada has many dilapidated colonial buildings, nearly all of which have at their center a patio where children play, figs ripen, and parrots squawk. But, as in Masaya, what is most appealing about Granada lies outside the city. Just west of its shore are a hundred or so tiny islands. It is said that Mombacho, the volcano that towers over Granada, blew off its erstwhile lake-facing side, creating the outcroppings. The Nicaraguan upper class has long used the *isletas* as weekend retreats, building Swiss-Family-Robinson-style cottages on them. A couple of the islands have restaurants, where iguana stew and *guapote,* a prized whitefish, are served. A motorboat taxi service links the islands.

A more ambitious outing is the four-hour drive north to León, much of it through rocky scrub (what Nicaraguan peasants call iguana land). Deservedly, the area is bereft of settlement, but nonetheless it is not unusual to

speed past a solitary boy standing at the edge of the highway, holding up for sale a chicken, or, more likely, a freshly killed iguana. As you approach León (which means lion in Spanish) the land becomes fertile and the region's volcanos come into view.

Unless you have family in León, there is nothing in the city of interest. The city does have an enormous cathedral, guarded by two haughty stone lions. The proffered explanation for why such a colonial backwater has such a cavernous cathedral is that the Spanish crown accidentally sent to León the design intended for Lima's cathedral. Supposedly, Lima in turn received the blueprints destined for León (thus explaining the tiny size of that city's cathedral). Since León never had any of Lima's gold, León's cathedral, while expansive, is austere. Modernity has brought fluorescent lights and plastic flowers. On my last visit to the cathedral, the robed priest at the door was stone drunk.

Just outside of León is a more arresting church, Sutiava. It is the oldest church in Nicaragua. Supposedly, the celebrated Spanish priest, Bartolomé de las Casas, preached from its pulpit prior to his 1547 departure from the Americas. The center of the forty-foot-high ceiling is adorned with a smiling sun. Legend has it that the Indians would not enter the church upon its completion because it had nothing to do with their deity. To gain a laity the Spanish friars were obliged to paint the vivid sun.

I climbed many of the towering volcanos surrounding León with my friend Tom and his two Ethiopian sons. There are no access roads to the volcanos, but Tom had a sturdy, old English Land Rover that would take us to their base. Climbing Cerro Negro is difficult because the volcano is nothing but loose, black sand. Despite the complete absence of vegetation, at the top of Cerro Negro

we were greeted by a porcupine, too crazed or weak to flee our presence. Telica is easier to climb, and the crater—the sight of which is always the reward for climbing a volcano—more exotic, giving you the eerie sensation of peering into someone's mind. At the foot of Telica are geysers and pools of boiling mud. In all, Nicaragua has twenty-five volcanos, eight of which are supposedly active. Climbing them is fun.

While Nicaragua's two most important colonial cities have Spanish names, small settlements often have names bequeathed by the all-but-vanquished Indians. The names are colorful: Niquinohomo, Nandaime, Masachapa, Nandayosi, Masatepe. These and similarly sized cities are not often visited. There is somewhat of a tradition in

Managua, though, of driving to Masatepe on a lazy Sunday for a brunch of *mondongo* (tripe soup) and rum. Another small town sometimes visited is Ciudad Darío, originally known as Metapa. The change in name was to honor Nicaragua's contribution to poetry, Rubén Darío. His home of birth there is a shrine.

Driving outside of Managua is pleasant, even idyllic. More so than elsewhere, the rhythm of life is slower outside the capital. And not only are there places to go, but sometimes the journey itself turns up surprises, of one sort or another. Once when returning from my favorite beach, Casares, I came upon a dozen men on horseback. They had tied a duck by its feet to a taut rope strung between two trees. The poor duck was perhaps fifteen feet off the ground, quacking incessantly. The men took turns galloping toward the duck, trying to pull its head off as they passed it. I did not stay to see which cowboy would be the winner.

On another outing, on the new road to León, the surprise was a big pig. Friends and I stopped at a roadside restaurant where the specialty was *quesillos* (tortillas wrapped around onions and cream), washed down with *tiste* (a beverage made from toasted maize and cacao). The latter was served in quaint gourds while the former was served in plastic bags. Once emptied, the gourds were returned to the waitress while the plastic bags, gooey with cream, were thrown on the dirt floor. One of the largest pigs I have ever seen walked around the tables eating the plastic bags.

INCAE

AT A MEETING in 1963 with Central American leaders, President Kennedy was asked if he could assist in the development of an institute to train the managers needed to run the region's growing, and modernizing, economies. After the meeting, President Kennedy asked the dean of the Harvard Business School to send a mission to the isthmus to explore the feasibility of such a project. The survey, under the direction of George Cabot Lodge, eventually led to a commitment by the Harvard Business School and the U.S. government to establish a high quality graduate school of management in Central America.

The result was the Instituto Centroamericano de Administración de Empresas, better known by its acronym, INCAE. (In Central America long names are given to entities so that their purpose is absolutely clear, but since the names are unwieldy, acronyms are used—which leaves the uninitiated with no clue as to what's what.) Teaching began in a hotel in Antigua, Guatemala. After spirited competition among the five Central American countries, Nicaragua was chosen to be INCAE's home. A group of landowners offered a magnificent tract of land for the campus on the outskirts of Managua. The U.S. Agency for International Development provided four million dollars. The Harvard Business School provided faculty, its case study teaching methodology, and Ivy League patina. The campus is spacious and freshened by cool breezes. It has well manicured grounds and a dazzling view of Managua, Lake Managua, and Momotombo. In addition to classrooms and offices, there are whitewashed bungalows capped with red tile roofs for resident faculty and students. The cement slab formerly used for drying coffee beans was turned into a basketball court, and the circular basin once used for washing the beans was converted into a delightful swimming pool, ringed with palm and mango trees. Behind the campus is a parcel still planted in coffee. Even farther back is a cave with pre-Columbian stickmen chiseled into the stone walls and overhang.

From its inception, INCAE enjoyed celebrated success. Hundreds of students graduated from its two-year M.B.A. program. Its six-week advanced management program was popular with executives. Students even began arriving from South America and Spain.

There was criticism, however. In 1975 a Sandinista guerrilla leader, Jaime Wheelock, published a book in Mexico, titled *Nicaragua: Imperialismo y Dictadura*, in which he damned INCAE for "teaching the methods and techniques of capitalist exploitation." INCAE was the advance guard of "*imperialismo yanqui.*"

I read Wheelock's book in preparation for my first visit to Nicaragua—and to INCAE, where I would work. When I arrived (in 1981), though, *Comandante* Wheelock, who with the triumph of the Revolution had been appointed Minister of Agricultural Development and Agrarian Reform, had become INCAE's best customer. He was sending many of his functionaries to established programs, and soliciting the design of a new program exclusively for the cadres who managed the vast agrarian estates taken from Somoza and his cronies. (These properties comprised one-fourth of Nicaragua's cultivated land!)

For INCAE, the Nicaraguan Revolution engendered many problems, including the difficulty of retaining faculty and recruiting students from other Central American countries. But INCAE did not want either to lose its pristine campus or to flinch from its self-imposed man-date to serve all of Central America. The outcome: in 1984 it opened a second campus outside of San José, Costa Rica, while still maintaining its Nicaraguan cam-pus. The M.B.A. program was transferred to Costa Rica, replaced in Nicaragua by an intensive one-year program in "functional" administration.

Even after the Costa Rican campus opened, I always returned to the Nicaraguan campus. My frequent trips to Nicaragua became synonymous with a stint at INCAE, where I had a bed, friends, and a parking lot for my Fiat. Usually at INCAE I worked on sponsored research proj-ects, always my preference over teaching. But once I did teach a semester-long course. There were ninety-six stu-dents in the class, mostly Nicaraguan, half of whom sup-ported—and worked for—the government. The other half ranged from ambivalence to disdain in their attitude towards the regime. In class, the students respectfully ad-dressed me as "Doctor." Outside class, I was nicknamed "Palo Alto," the elegant translation being "Tall Sapling" (I am tall). Alas, the more common meaning is "Big Stick." The nickname had an edge to it: Managua's most notorious jail is also named Palo Alto. I did not mind being called "Big Stick" because it seemed infinitely better than the fate of one of my students, who was dubbed what his head supposedly resembled—cabbage.

It never was clear to me what contribution my bright and eager students would make to Nicaragua. I guessed that at least some would leave the country. There were opportunities, though, for those who elected to stay. The flight of so many managers had left gaping holes in many

firms. And the Sandinistas' elephantine bureaucracies provided countless jobs. Yet even for those who stayed, the potential contribution was murky. The administrative environment was daunting, not only because of the poverty of resources, but also because the Revolution obscured how the workplace—public and private—should be managed.

Comandante Wheelock came to INCAE one evening to address a group of his administrators who were studying there. I went. Wheelock was visibly tired and spoke solemnly. At one point he lowered his voice and said, "This is a North American institution, with its ties to Harvard." He paused, looked at me, and said, in an even lower voice, "You can learn something from the North Americans." A couple of minutes later, though, he said that the formal study of administration was good, but what was needed was "revolutionary solutions." The closest he came to defining this alternative was his assertion that administration has to have "historical content." I was confused, and so, I suspected, was everyone else.

The Carretera Sur

MY LINK BETWEEN INCAE and Managua, and Nicaragua at large, was the Carretera Sur, the South Highway. It is the local name for what is actually the Pan American Highway. If INCAE was my home, the Carretera Sur was my neighborhood.

The neighborhood begins just outside of INCAE's boundaries. The Instituto is set in a kilometer from the Carretera Sur. Upon its establishment a developer bought the land between the Instituto and the highway and laid out a grid for a wealthy community. Short, interlacing streets were constructed and paved with large cobblestones. Concrete monuments at the intersections reveal that the streets are named after the famous universities of the world, for example, Stanford, the Sorbonne, and the National Autonomous University of Nicaragua (UNAN). Some wealthy Nicaraguans built pricey homes on the expansive and well-shaded lots.

With the Revolution, however, all such construction halted. Slowly, poor, landless peasants, unafraid of eviction, homesteaded the remaining lots. They built shacks and sowed, not flowers and shrubbery, but corn and beans.

The result is the most curious borough: a checkerboard of mansions and hovels, of pigs and Mercedes Benzes, of manicured lawns on Princeton and cornstalks on Yale.

Out on the Carretera Sur one finds the same contrast between wealth and poverty. Because of the altitude, vegetation is profuse and exuberant. But tucked among the trees, bushes, plantains, and coffee are homes. Many of the homes are large, luxurious, and surrounded by fences, walls, and gates. Sometimes signs on or above the gates identify the fantasies of the owners: they announce, for example, "Camelot" or "Villa Roma." Interspaced at unpredictable intervals are the homes of the less fortunate. They are not surrounded by fences or walls.

But on the Carretera Sur there are more than houses. Driving down the highway from INCAE to Managua, I would pass, in order: a colony of Cubans, the Honduran Embassy, a militia headquarters, the Monte Tabor Catholic Church, the Becklin residential colony, the Parador Campestre restaurant, a post office, the Calsanz Catholic School, the Brazilian Embassy, the Walter Mendoza Martínez police academy, an FSLN office, the Comandante Eduardo Contreras Disciplinary Complex, an Esso gas station, the Wilmar whore house, a traffic inspection office, the Hotel Ticomo (Triple AAA), the Típico Habana Inn Restaurant-Discotec Night Club, the Mini-Super Licorería, the 7Up Miscelánea store, the Tucán restaurant, and, finally, a Shell gas station.

For me, Managua begins at the Shell station. From there you can see Motastepe, the pyramid-shaped hill adorned with four huge, white letters: FSLN. At the Siete Sur intersection you can turn right onto the By-

Pass or you can continue straight ahead. Either way, you are in Managua.

Traffic along the Carretera Sur is not heavy, yet one of the favorite topics of conversation in the neighborhood is traffic accidents. They usually involve at least one of three hazards: oxen-pulled carts hauling firewood into Managua, cattle, or drunks. The most spectacular accident I saw, though, was when an IFA army truck missed a curve, rolled up an earthen bank, and smashed into the Monte Tabor church.

Another favorite topic of discussion, among rich and poor alike, is government confiscation of property. The most talked-about confiscation was of the most valuable property—the Becklin colony, consisting of twenty-two opulent houses and seven apartments. The colony was owned by Señora Becklin, a widow. She had been married to a U.S. Marine but was herself a member of the González family, a very rich family but one that had been in opposition to Somoza. The colony was abruptly confiscated but for reasons that were never clear. Speculation ensued up and down the Carretera Sur. Someone said the colony was confiscated because Señora Becklin had been married to a Marine. Someone else claimed it was because she was a González. Another suggested the Sandinistas needed a big place for foreigners.

I kept abreast of the Carretera Sur in part by picking up hitchhikers on my way up to INCAE. Some I came to know reasonably well. The Siete Sur intersection is always mobbed with hitchhikers, but unless I recognized someone I usually did not stop. Most people wanted to go further than INCAE, to the towns of Carazo, Jino-

tepe, or Diriamba. And anyway, my Fiat had a hard
enough time climbing the Carretera Sur.

Coming down the Carretera Sur from INCAE to Managua was a different matter. I stopped for everyone,
sometimes even if they did not have their thumb ex-
tended. Some barefoot old men I picked up had never
been in a car before—only on a bus. The most memorable hitchhiker I encountered was a peasant clutching a
handsome rooster. He earned his living growing corn
and beans, picking coffee, and doing odd jobs as they appeared. His love was cockfighting, which he explained
with great gusto. Cockfighting was not what it was before the Revolution, but in those days poor peasants like
him could not afford purebred roosters. With the Revolution, many rich men had left the country but had left
behind their cocks.

Pregnancy

WITHIN MY FIRST TWO WEEKS in Nicaragua I was
rattled by a gorgeous Nicaraguan woman. Upon my being introduced to her, she abruptly asked me, "Where
are you from?"

"The United States."

"You know you North Americans are really clever at
inventing all kinds of machines and gadgets, but there
are two things you can't do. You can't dance and you are
no good in bed."

I did not say anything because I knew I did not know
how to dance.

In time, though, I learned how to dance, if only badly.
And I came to decide that the notion of Nicaraguans as
talented Latin lovers was a myth. Foreplay seemed to
consist of little more than a few kisses and a shared beer.
A gynecologist confirmed my impression. She said only a
small percentage of Nicaraguan women ever have or-
gasms. There are women who have borne twelve children and never experienced an orgasm.

Fathoming just how the status of Nicaraguan women
has changed with the Revolution is elusive. The Revolu-

tion was fought to oust a dictator and to attack class divisions. But the larger goal was to provide a better life for all Nicaraguans, particularly the majority who had long been marginalized. Women are prominent in this poor majority. Similarly, while the Revolution immediately—and most visibly—overturned a government and shook the prevailing economic order, more globally it questioned *mentalités,* customs, and conventions. And deeply ingrained in Nicaraguans are conceptions about how they are most obviously divided—by gender. An outline of this division is suggested by the Nicaraguan expression, "The man is king of the street; the woman is queen of the house."

What would the Sandinistas do to improve the lives of women? Would they be absorbed in forming a new state, running a weak and badgered economy, and defending themselves against a counterrevolution? If there was room on the revolutionary agenda for women, what could be done, given the generalized poverty of resources in the country? More unsettling, were the vexatious problems of Nicaraguan women even amenable to solution by government policies and programs?

The ranking positions in both the Sandinista party and the government are filled by men. The Sandinista National Directorate is all male. There is only one ministry (the Ministry of Health) headed by a woman. The overwhelming majority of women employed in government are secretaries and janitors. But an articulate group of women organized themselves into the Nicaraguan Women's Association (AMNLAE). While they are counted as a Sandinista "mass organization" and are instrumental in mobilizing support for the regime, they also lobby for the welfare of women.

On numerous occasions, ranking Sandinistas have committed themselves to improving the status of women. But no specific plan has ever emerged. AMNLAE has done no better. Nonetheless, between themselves, AMNLAE and the government have accomplished some things. Pornography has been outlawed, as have been advertisements that degrade women. The Civil Code has been amended to make women's participation in the family and the economy fairer. Some day care centers have been established. Rapists are prosecuted more vigorously. Moreover, the sheer presence of the Revolution has weakened traditional male prerogatives in the family and the workplace. It is less easy for privilege to be defended with the justification, "That's the way it always has been."

Sometimes there have been surprises, though. For example, the November 24, 1988, issue of *Barricada* announced the first "Miss Teenager" beauty contest. There were pictures of the 15- and 16-year-old candidates. The accompanying article described one teenager from Estelí as a "pretty pine cone," and quoted another aspirant as saying she looked forward to the bathing suit parade because of her "visible advantages." The prize for the winner was an all-expense-paid trip to North Korea to attend the World Youth and Student Festival. The article closed by announcing that soldiers would enter the contest grounds free of charge and men presenting their draft cards would pay half-price.

My perception of how Nicaraguan women have fared with the Revolution has been formed by the sad story of my friend Denia. When I met her she was an economist with the national electricity company. She lived at home with her idle parents, a lazy cousin waiting for her newlywed husband to return from soldiering, and two young twins who had been left with the household by indeterminate relatives. Denia and her hardworking brother, a truck driver, supported the household.

In Nicaragua you can discern the class membership of a family by the floor of their home. The poor have dirt, the middle class have cement, and the wealthy tile or parquet. Denia's house had a cement floor, a tin roof, bare light bulbs, and a television. With her university degree and professional employment, Denia was the pride of the family.

Denia and I drove all over Managua in my Fiat, enjoying what the city and my dollars had to offer. We became close, but when I left Nicaragua we parted only as esteemed friends.

When I returned to Nicaragua, maybe six months later, I visited Denia. Over dinner she told me she was involved with a man and that, in fact, they were planning to marry. He was a jealous Nicaraguan, so it was best if I no longer came to the house.

I did not see Denia again until my next visit to Managua. I could not resist visiting her, although I was worried that she had married and was at home with her jealous husband. Her mother welcomed me into the house, informing me that yes, Denia had married, and even had a baby, and yes, she was at home, but no, her husband was not there. Denia came out from the inner recesses of the house. During our conversation she said her husband was up north, in León, working. But when she went to get her baby to show me, her mother told me it was all a lie, that two weeks after the birth of the boy, Denia had come home, separated from her husband. The husband was no good, irresponsible, a drunkard. When Denia returned with her baby she seemed to know I knew the truth. As I left, her mother said it was a shame Denia and I had not gotten married, but that I was the type of man who wanted to wait until I was fifty years old to get married. While driving back to INCAE I figured out from the date of the baby's birth that Denia had gotten pregnant unintentionally, and was pushed into the ill-fated marriage.

I did not see Denia or her family for close to two years, despite visiting Managua during the period.

When I went back to the house I knew so well, her

mother warmly greeted me but had disturbing news. Denia had started seeing her husband again, had gotten
pregnant, and so was living with him, trying to make a
go of the marriage. I said to give her my regards and left.

Two days later Denia called and asked me to come
visit her during the day, while her husband was at work.
She looked very pregnant and very depressed. She no
longer worked. Her husband objected to that and, anyway, she had to take care of her son. She was alone a lot;
he did not come home until late. And they quarreled.

Thinking about Denia later, I was reminded of what a Nicaraguan vegetable vendor once told me, "The problem with Nicaraguan men is that they father children and then leave." I agree. A man's fleeting pleasure can, if it leads to pregnancy, irrevocably change a woman's life. And Nicaraguan women give birth to an average of six children. Unhappily, the problem is hardly amenable to a solution initiated and implemented by government. It is good to amend laws, but even just laws seemingly cannot alter the traditional and continuing vulnerability of women. And, besides, only an estimated one-sixth of Nicaraguan marriages are civil or church-sanctified agreements.

Róger had an illuminating, if sober, cartoon in *Barricada*. A man leaning against a wall calls out to his wife, "The child fell down!" From inside the house the wife yells, "So tell the government to pick him up!"

Orlando's Ranch

AT INCAE I MET the director of one of Nicaragua's state enterprises, the Marcos Somarriba Enterprise. After a few spirited discussions, the bearded director, Orlando, invited me to see his firm, located in an isolated corner of Nicaragua. I accepted his offer with enthusiasm.

Managua is the demographic, political, and cultural center of Nicaragua. It is home to a fourth of Nicaraguans, including all of the *políticos*. But Nicaragua remains an agrarian country. Nearly half of the populace earn their living from the land. More importantly, 90 percent of the exports so crucial to a small economy are derived from agriculture. What happens in the capital determines the country's political tack; what happens in the countryside determines the health of the country's economy.

A visit to one of the stated economic vanguards of the Revolution was irresistible. And I had never been to Río San Juan, home of the Marcos Somarriba Enterprise.

After a bus ride to Granada, I took a "speedboat" across the length of Lake Nicaragua. Speedy as the boat was, it was seven hours before I was shaking Orlando's hand once again. From that moment, he began to tell me the tale of the Marcos Somarriba Enterprise.

The most isolated and neglected region of Nicaragua is the Department of the San Juan River. Western Nicaragua, where the bulk of the country's population lives, is marked by a cordillera of volcanos linking the Gulf of Fonseca in the north and Lake Nicaragua in the south. These volcanos protrude from a large rift that forms a long, narrow depression. The rift is occupied in part by the largest freshwater lakes in Central America: Lake Managua (56 kilometers long and 24 kilometers wide) and Lake Nicaragua (161 kilometers long and 75 kilometers wide). These two lakes are linked by the Tipitapa River. The southernmost lake, Lake Nicaragua, drains into the San Juan River, which flows to the Caribbean. For some of its length, the river serves as the boundary between Nicaragua and Costa Rica.

The San Juan Valley forms a natural low-lying passageway across the Nicaraguan isthmus from the Caribbean Sea to Lake Nicaragua. From the southwest edge of Lake Nicaragua it is then only nineteen kilometers to the Pacific Ocean. During the 1850s, the Panama route was the most popular way to transit between the Atlantic and Pacific coasts of the United States, but it was challenged for a few years by the shorter, cheaper, and healthier Nicaragua route. Since Nicaragua's latitude was higher, the climate was said to be cooler, and passengers were less exposed to the risk of tropical fevers. None other than Cornelius Vanderbilt ran the transit company shuttling passengers from coast to coast. Mark Twain made the trip in 1866 and described it as a "jolly little scamper across the isthmus."

Engineers had always considered this Nicaraguan route as the most practical site for a transisthmian canal. At several times designs were drawn up, but each time they were frustrated by political squabbling. It was only be-cause of politics in the end that the canal was built in Panama.

With the construction of the transisthmus Panama-nian railway and later the canal itself, the San Juan River fell into oblivion. The valley was never colonized, and the settlements at either end of the river—San Car-los on Lake Nicaragua and San Juan del Norte on the Caribbean—remained small shantytowns. After World War II, cattle ranches were slowly established through the burning off and clearing of the tropical forest. The area remained inaccessible to overland vehicles, with transportation limited to boats plying the lake and the river. The seven ranches that hugged the river reached enormous size, but stretched only a third of the way to-ward the coast. A few laborers managed large herds of cattle, which grazed at will, as if they were in the wild. Ranches were also established on some of the larger is-lands near the southeastern end of Lake Nicaragua.

The somnolence of the San Juan Valley ended with the Nicaraguan Revolution. There was little fighting in the region (although arms and supplies were ferried across the river from Costa Rica). With the triumph of the Sandinista insurrection, however, ownership of the entire valley passed to the State. Most of the land in the area was affected by the initial decrees confiscating the assets of Somoza and his associates. *El General,* as

Somoza is referred to in the region, is said to have been the largest landowner. Other land is said to have been abandoned at the onset of the Sandinista's "final offensive." The owners never returned, leaving the land to be appropriated by the State.

An organization was hastily established by the revolutionary government to manage and develop all the land in the San Juan Valley. The organization, the Río San Juan Enterprise, was based in San Carlos under the jurisdiction of the Ministry of Agricultural Development and Agrarian Reform. It was responsible for an enormous tract of land, much of which was covered with tropical forest, especially near the Caribbean coast. Attention centered on the cattle ranches. All of the farms had been owned by absentee landlords, facilitating their occupation by the revolutionary government. There was no sabotage, but some livestock is believed to have been spirited across the Costa Rican border.

The Río San Juan Enterprise was also given control over a number of small ranches on the islands in Lake Nicaragua which lie close to San Carlos. In addition, the firm was given a few unsettled cays and an island planted entirely in avocados, which are watered by a well-developed irrigation system. No one seems to remember who owned the latter other than that he was "a famous millionaire."

The Río San Juan Enterprise was hastily organized, but it managed rather quickly to establish a sense of order on the confiscated estates. Anarchy was avoidable because of the simplicity of the estates' activity and the permanence of many workers who knew more or less what to do. Work slowed, to be sure, and such activities as mending fences came to a virtual halt. No thought was given to using the estates for anything other than cattle grazing, but there was a great deal of uncertainty as to how they would be managed. In fact, exactly how the enterprise was to be organized and managed was never defined. The firm had no specific objectives, and no strategy. Decisions were made on a day-to-day basis, with little effort at continuity. The state financial system provided funding to stimulate production, and the money was simply spent as problems arose. No one bothered to keep records of any kind. Personnel came and went, with many administrations staying for only two or three months. The firm's first director himself abruptly fled to Costa Rica.

For three years, the company operated without any accounting system at all. Consequently, it was impossible to know whether the enterprise was efficiently using the resources with which it had been entrusted. Finally, in the middle of 1982, a team of auditors and accountants arrived from Managua. They pieced together a balance statement and set up an accounting system. The balance statement revealed a large debt to the nationalized bank. A small part of the debt had been inherited from the confiscated farms, and another part represented investments, but the majority of the debt was deemed to be an unrecoverable loss from the initial three years of state management.

In late 1983, the Ministry of Agricultural Development and Agrarian Reform, believing that the enterprise was simply too large, divided it into two. The undeveloped eastern half was reorganized into a new firm named Hilario Sánchez. The cattle estates centering around San Carlos were to be retained under the Río San Juan Enterprise, but the now leaner enterprise was renamed Commander Marcos Somarriba. While the assets of the Río San Juan Enterprise were divided between the two entities, the Marcos Somarriba firm was saddled with all of its debt.

Even after the split, the reorganized firm at San Carlos is huge. It possesses 60,000 hectares, making it one of the largest agricultural enterprises (in terms of area) in Nicaragua. Slightly over half the land consists of uncleared brush or forest. Roughly a third is in pasture, the bulk of it cultivated. Most of the remaining land is cleared of brush, but fallow. Only a fraction of one percent of the total land is planted in perennial and annual crops. The former include cacao and avocado, while the latter are mostly vegetables.

Since its inception the enterprise has maintained about 16,500 head of cattle. There is enough land, though, to quadruple the herd.

The firm is organized into three complexes. Each complex, in turn, is made up of Production Enterprise Units (UPEs, pronounced oopays) that are productively similar and/or are in close proximity to one another. For example, one complex is composed of two large cattle ranches that are close enough to San Carlos to be accessible by land, facilitating the use of agricultural machinery. A second complex consists of the other five cattle ranches, spread out along the San Juan River from its banks to the Costa Rican border. The third complex groups together the island farms in the lake. Two of its UPEs are cattle ranches; the other five are devoted to permanent and annual crops. Each of the three complexes is administratively centered in an UPE—the one that has the best living conditions.

Little was inherited in the way of infrastructure when the estates were confiscated. To be sure, there were barbed-wire fences, horses, and a few corrals. The largest estate did have some equipment, an above-ground fuel tank, boats of varying sizes, assorted buildings, an elegant home overlooking the river, and a pet jaguar (chained to a stake, of course). Another estate had a large comfortable home which was used by the former owner during his visits. The remaining estates had only slovenly quarters for the few workers who tended the cattle. Since the Revolution, the beautiful home with the pet jaguar has been designated as a protocol residence for visiting government dignitaries. (The jaguar is still chained to the stake.) The other large home is used as a Sandinista school for the political training of cadres.

What the enterprise did find itself with of value was an eclectic array of boats. Most important was a large vessel, apparently built to haul vehicles. A wide gate at the bow lowers to serve as a bridge into the open hull. The boat also tugs a barge that functions as a sort of floating metal corral. Together the two craft can transport seventy head of cattle to Granada. The trip takes from twenty-five to thirty hours, depending on the weather.

The enterprise also inherited half a dozen smaller boats, each with a different brand of outboard motor. These provide transportation among the enterprise's

UPEs, and between the San Juan Valley and the more populous Pacific zone of Nicaragua. There is also a beat-up Suzuki jeep, but it is only good for visiting two of the UPEs, and even for that it is slower than a boat.

Comparable to the poverty of infrastructure (in not only absolute terms, but also in comparison with the Pacific zone), is the paucity of labor in general, and the near absence of educated labor in particular. While some of the manual laborers were reached by the Sandinista literacy campaign, nearly all seemed to have returned to functional illiteracy, unable to do more than sign their name. Many of the local workers relocate periodically. Few share the attitude of one who told me, "There is no point in moving around because you eat rice and beans in every *hacienda.* "

An especially serious problem is the flight of workers to Costa Rica, who reportedly leave for economic, not political, reasons. Laborers claim that they can buy a pair of pants with two days' earnings in Costa Rica, whereas for the same pair of pants they would have to work a month in Nicaragua. A few have fled to Costa Rica to avoid Nicaragua's obligatory military service. Laborers from elsewhere in Nicaragua have reportedly come to work for the enterprise in order to use it as a "trampoline" to cross into Costa Rica.

By all accounts, laborers in the valley have little interest in politics. As is said by local Sandinista cadres, they have an "underdeveloped political consciousness." Workers are held to be hardy and brave, but occupied primarily with selfish concerns. Despite the reorganization of the ranches into a state enterprise, the workers do not seem to feel that their situation has changed very much since the Revolution. The farms are routinely referred to as *haciendas,* just as the director of the UPE is referred to as the *patrón.* More importantly, workers are not interested in the profitability of the enterprise, since they earn the same no matter what the firm earns—or loses. The workers' lack of education and political consciousness is yet another difficulty engendered by the historical isolation and neglect of the San Juan Valley.

Management of the Marcos Somarriba Enterprise is made even more troublesome by counterrevolutionary forces. Guerrilla bands have penetrated as far as the outskirts of San Carlos. In 1983 an attack was launched on the firm's most important UPE, resulting in heavy losses. In early 1985, Orlando and four of his staff were caught in an ambush; there were no fatalities, but the manager of an UPE was wounded. A more constant problem has been the theft of cattle, especially from UPEs bordering Costa Rica. By 1985 the cumulative loss was estimated at 1,500 cattle.

The counterrevolution has not only wrought direct losses to the firm, but has also created a climate of fear and uncertainty that exacts a cost even when all appears normal. Many employees of the firm, especially administrators, have received instruction in the handling of weapons, and UPEs always have AK-47s at the ready. Not surprisingly, recruiting personnel outside of the valley to work at the enterprise is nearly impossible. A typical response is: "No, brother, I'm not bored with life yet."

To meet the threat of the counterrevolution the Sandinista army has staged small contingents of troops at several of the firm's UPEs, in particular those bordering Costa Rica. The troops serve both to deter the advance of guerrilla columns and to protect employees and infrastructure. They improvise their own shelter, which is rarely more than a simple roof of some sort, since they sleep in hammocks. They are fed by the enterprise, though, and eat with the workers. The practice of stationing troops at UPEs is common along both the northern and southern borders of the country.

The firm would never seek to impede the deployment of the Sandinista army, since defense is unquestionably paramount. A common slogan in postrevolutionary Nicaragua is "Everything for Defense." Still, the stationing of troops at the firm's UPEs is a mixed blessing. It is unclear whether the presence of troops thwarts or invites attacks by guerrillas on state farms; the evidence is mixed. Laborers at Marcos Somarriba's UPEs will not venture into unsettled areas with the troops, nor will they carry arms. Less consequential, but of importance nonetheless, are the petty problems caused by the troops: the extra expense and chore of supplying provisions, the occasional quarrel between a soldier and a laborer, and such nuisances as the shooting of a prized bull by a bored soldier.

Perhaps because of its difficult environment, the Marcos Somarriba firm has experienced high turnover among administrative personnel. In its first five years it has had four directors, one of whom supposedly was so taken back by the problems in the UPEs that he would not leave his office in San Carlos. Likewise, the firm has had five head accountants, and similar turnover has occurred at the UPEs. The high rotation of administrators has made it difficult to address the urgent problems facing the enterprise, or even to devise ways of living with them.

In 1985 the firm found some stability with the appointment of Orlando, a veterinarian, as Director. Although he had no prior experience in administration, his family owned and managed a cattle ranch in the Department of Boaco. Perhaps of equal importance to the Minister, who appoints directors, Orlando is a member of the Front for Sandinista National Liberation. Upon his appointment, Orlando sought the help of several of his friends who had been cattle ranchers in Boaco until they were displaced by the fighting between the Sandinista army and the counterrevolutionaries. His most trusted friend assumed the position of Manager of Production, while others became directors of the most productive UPEs.

The arrival of Orlando's friends evoked considerable criticism from employees. He has been charged with *amigoísmo* and *boacoísmo*. Still, it is readily apparent that the Boacoans are experienced cattle ranchers and hard workers. Ironically, except for Orlando himself, the Boacoans do not have a strong political commitment to the Revolution. They are cattle ranchers who simply feel displaced anywhere else than on a cattle ranch. One confided his hope that by working on a government farm he would improve his chances of getting his ranch back once the government had cleared the counterrevolutionaries out of Boaco and the neighboring departments of Chontales and Zelaya.

Even with a staff of thirty-seven at the firm's headquarters and personnel at each UPE, Orlando spends most days out in the countryside. He attempts to stay personally on top of each UPE's progress and problems. Often he and his "right hand," the production manager, will leave San Carlos in the morning by boat, taking their saddles and Orlando's AK-47, and spend the day on a special task at an UPE. A common task is the transfer of cattle from one area to another. Orlando thus spends much of his time doing the work of an ordinary field hand, staying in touch with whatever is going on in the fields.

Orlando avoids spending time in his office because "it is boring" and because he prefers to devote his time to what he sees as the firm's central objective—to raise live-stock. Administrative tasks are judged to be bothersome and cumbersome. Worse, there are constant interruptions. For example, one day a stranger walked into his office with a sizeable check from the enterprise that had bounced. The check had been written a year and a half earlier, before Orlando had even assumed management of the firm. When the bank finally finished processing the check, there was not enough money in the firm's account to cover it. Orlando had to spend the better part of a day negotiating with the bank to make the check good.

Nominally the firm's activities are guided by an annual plan, the Technical Economic Plan (PTE). A number of individuals in the Department of Economics devote considerable time to drawing up the plan, with the administrators of the UPEs also contributing to the process. Yet the plan is used only to secure financing from the local branch of the National Development Bank. Once the year's financing has been received, the PTE is all but forgotten. Projected costs are based on actual costs at the time of the plan, but inflation quickly wreaks havoc with the financial side of the PTE, making it useless as a budget. The production goals established in the PTE should, it would seem, serve as a guide to the management of the enterprise, but in actuality they are virtually ignored.

Nonetheless, the firm collects a formidable amount of information, most of it purportedly for control purposes. But while Orlando has available to him statistical data to complement what he sees on his visits to the country-side, he does not have information on the financial return of productive activity. Consequently, there is no guide as to what to do, or what not to do and, probably more seriously, no factual basis for setting priorities in the allocation of resources.

The belated establishment of an accounting department finally enabled the firm to get an idea of the financial results of its operations, and held forth the promise of providing information for managerial decision making. The first income statement prepared was for the 1982/1983 agricultural season. The recorded balance for the firm's third year of operations was a loss of seven million *córdobas;* however, roughly four million worth of supposed accounts receivable never materialized, so that the

actual net loss was eleven million *córdobas*. Income and expenses were managed in a single account, or "single bag" in the vernacular, which made it impossible to identify why or where the firm lost money.

At the end of the 1983/1984 agricultural season, the enterprise benefited from the arrival of a skilled and dedicated accountant, Francisco. He struggled to bring the accounting up to date and to improve its reliability. Equally important, he began to break down costs by UPE and by activity. When he had assembled total costs per UPE for the 1983/1984 agricultural season, the accounting department constructed a huge matrix on a roll of newsprint. Measuring four feet by ten feet, the matrix was the central attraction at a large meeting for the firm's employees in San Carlos and for special invitees. There was a sense of accomplishment; for the first time, the firm knew where its money was going. The residents of San Carlos who attended the presentation were said to be impressed too, with someone claiming, "We thought you had been spending the money like it was from a *piñata* and stealing it like whores."

Francisco prepared the year's income statement in an unorthodox way, but in a manner that showed how each of the firm's activities contributed to the year's results. The bottom line was a loss of nearly seven million *córdobas* on sales of eleven million *córdobas*—a shocking ratio. Administration accounted for a staggering 37 percent of total costs.

A continued weakness of the firm's accounting is that costs are equated only with cash outlays. Thus, when cattle are stolen or lost, the corresponding cost is not entered into the firm's accounts. Given the magnitude of cattle thefts from the firm, this omission is consequential. Orlando is convinced that the drubbing the Sandinista army gave local counterrevolutionaries in 1985 will end the problem, but even an occasional "stray loss" should be recorded and entered into the calculation of the firm's annual income statement.

A similar confusion exists over depreciation. The firm does not depreciate at all the assets acquired through confiscation of the estates that make up the firm. Its investments in machinery are depreciated, but in an arbitrary fashion. For example, the largest and most productive UPE acquired seven new Belrusa tractors at the start of the 1984/1985 agricultural season. Six months later, three of them were more or less permanently out of service, with one being cannibalized for spare parts. According to the UPE's mechanic, the problem is that the Soviet tractors are "shitty," while Orlando claims, "The firm's mechanics only know how to destroy equipment, not fix it." In any case, no special consideration is made in the firm's accounts for the loss of the machinery. Even the cannibalized tractor will be depreciated for another four years.

Despite such problems, the firm's accounting has improved considerably, but not to the point where accounting data can be used for managerial decision making. Comparison of production costs with revenue generated is especially difficult for the firm's principal activity— livestock. Cattle are kept by the firm for varying lengths of time, but almost always for more than a single agricultural cycle. How does one measure the value gained by having an animal grazing for a year? Beyond this inherent difficulty, there is the complication caused by the constant shuttling of animals from one UPE to another, which is made for obscure reasons. No record is kept of these transfers, making it impossible to even estimate the revenue generated by individual UPEs. Managers of UPEs not only do not know whether their particular UPEs are profitable, but they do not even know whether the firm itself makes or loses money. No one informs them.

Problems of interpreting the income statement for the 1983/1984 agricultural cycle were not taken too seriously by Orlando because, by the time the income statement was prepared, inflation had wrought havoc with prices. Costs had risen, but there was also a sense that liberalization of certain commodity prices by the central government would aid the firm. In particular, livestock prices were raised dramatically—by close to 100 percent. The rise was precipitated by the private sector's failure to deliver livestock to the nation's slaughterhouses, all of which are owned and operated by the government. An alarming share of the livestock was being slaughtered clandestinely and sold on the flourishing black market. To combat this trend, the government raised prices, even going to the extreme of paying a small fraction of the total price in U.S. dollars (paid in cash).

The price of cacao and avocados has also increased dramatically. For example, in two years the price paid to the firm for its avocados increased tenfold. Vegetable production, in contrast, is of concern. The cultivation of vegetables is not carried out directly by the firm. Instead it is part of a nationwide program for food self-sufficiency, known by its acronym PAN. The Marcos Somarriba Enterprise assumes financial responsibility for the program's local activities, but has next to no control over its management.

San Carlos and its environs are almost completely dependent on the shipment of food (and nearly everything else) across Lake Nicaragua from the populous Pacific departments. The leadership of the PAN program decided that San Carlos should begin to grow foodstuffs. To this end two small islands in Lake Nicaragua named after a tropical fruit, the zapote, were designated for the production of vegetables. A project director was appointed, and the Marcos Somarriba Enterprise was ordered to provide technical and financial assistance. The National Development Bank provided funding, but the loans were made to the firm, not the project.

After two years of work, the project had made considerable investments in the building of infrastructure. The project has difficulty hiring and keeping workers, though. On two occasions field workers have disappeared in the middle of the night, stealing one of the project's motorboats. As a consequence of labor shortages, only a fifth of the hectares planned for cultivation have actually been cultivated. Although the foreman (a fugitive Costa Rican) is knowledgeable and experienced, production has been low and of poor quality.

The project director claims that within a few years production will be improved to the point where it will cover costs. Orlando is doubtful. For him the project is a headache and a financial disaster. Perhaps a few crops that require little labor input, such as cassava and plantain, might ultimately prove profitable, but the results to date suggest the firm would be better off just abandoning the project. Aggravating these concerns is the realization that many costs incurred have not yet been recorded.

The dilemma posed by the PAN project is typical of those confronting Orlando. Supposedly, he is director of a firm, responsible to the Ministry of Agricultural Development and Agrarian Reform and to the National Development Bank for its financial success or failure. Yet he does not have the independence commensurate with such responsibility. The firm is burdened by obligations that have little or nothing to do with its central purpose—to produce livestock efficiently.

A similar problem exists with the firm's employees in San Carlos. Despite their relative advantage over workers in the countryside, they are always pressing Orlando to provide special benefits to them. In particular, they have long urged that the firm open a commissary providing necessary commodities at "rational prices," a euphemism for subsidized prices. Employees also commonly ask for loans. Even other residents of San Carlos ask for assorted favors that entail costs of one sort or another to the firm. Orlando's efforts to deny these requests have more than once elicited the retort that he is a capitalist.

Orlando, Director of Commander Marcos Somarriba, is deeply committed to the Revolution and the responsibility with which it has entrusted him. He aspires for the enterprise to become a vanguard firm, which he defines principally in terms of the political consciousness of its workers, but also in terms of productivity and efficiency. He views the counterrevolution, which presents indirect as well as direct costs to the firm, as his main obstacle. Symbolically, the largest drawer in his desk is filled with grenades. Despite Orlando's preoccupation with the counterrevolution, he strives continuously to improve the management of the firm.

The need to improve management stems largely from the firm's gloomy balance sheet. Perhaps surprisingly, Orlando's concern is his own; no one in the Ministry seems to evaluate the firm, let alone complain. The bank officials with whom he negotiates the firm's credit line are sometimes critical, but they always provide credit. Nonetheless, Orlando senses that it is harmful for a state enterprise to be continuously losing money. He is determined that people not joke, as they commonly do, that the state sector's acronym, APP, stands for *autorizado para perder* (authorized to be unprofitable).

Efforts to improve the management of the firm have resulted in everything from placing a large snake in the warehouse (to eat mice and deter thieves) to improving the accounting system. Perhaps most important, though, is establishing the firm as a productive entity. As Orlando put it, "People have to realize that the firm is not an army base, an employment agency, a store, or a bank—it is a cattle enterprise."

After saying *adiós* to Orlando, I boarded a ferry for the trip back to Granada. It left in the late afternoon, but was so slow that it would not arrive in Granada until late in the morning of the following day. Orlando had suggested I find a hammock below deck, but they were all taken by the time I boarded. I spent a miserable night sprawled out on the steel deck. My shoes served as my pillow, in part because I had been warned that the shoes of sleeping passengers are often stolen. Sleep was elusive—it rained intermittently and the deck was hard. While waiting for daylight, I wondered what the fortunes of the Enterprise Marcos Somarriba said about the possibilities for revolutionary change in a poor country. My mind kept returning to something Orlando said: "The Revolution is beautiful—it's the disorder that screws everything up."

In the morning, a fat woman wandered about the boat, announcing to everyone that a rogue had stolen her shoes during the night.

The Corn Islands

IN CENTRAL AMERICA the most important holiday stretches for a week—Semana Santa (Holy Week)—the week between Palm Sunday and Easter. As far as I can tell, though, the holiday is important because the week falls at the height of the dry season, the ideal time to go to the beach. And that is what Nicaraguans traditionally do (if they can afford it). No one does much swimming, but enormous quantities of rum are consumed and *chistes* (jokes) are told and retold.

After my tiring trip to the San Juan Valley, I felt I deserved a bit of luxury and so departed from the usual habit of spending Semana Santa at the Pacific. Instead I joined four friends, three Nicaraguans and an Italian, who were traveling to the distant Atlantic Coast, to Nicaragua's two most beautiful backwaters, the Corn Islands. The islands lie forty miles off the coast. Their name purportedly reflects the extensive corn fields of the original inhabitants, the Miskito Indians, but today it is a misnomer—not a single stalk of maize remains. Instead you see coconuts, endless forests of graceful palm trees bearing fruit. Most of the Miskitos have been replaced, too, largely by Afro-Americans who arrived via Jamaica. Although in the distant past these outcroppings were visited by lurid buccaneers, they eventually became an oasis of harmony. With circumferences of seven and five miles, respectively, Great Corn Island, until recently, had roughly seven thousand inhabitants and Little Corn Island a mere four hundred. There never were any fortunes to be made on either. Nonetheless, everyone had enough to eat as well as clean clothes in which to attend one of the numerous Protestant churches. And "nobody worried nobody."

I had visited the Corn Islands three years before, joining two women from Ecuador for a balmy Christmas. We had a pleasant visit. When I returned, though, a former suspicion hardened: under Sandinista rule, the quality of life on the islands has suffered a marked decline, underscored by the flight of nearly half the islanders. As tranquil as the islands were, my friends and I were again and again reminded of the difficulty of radical change amid poverty and isolation, especially when ethnic divisions complicate the endeavor.

Flights from Managua to the Corn Islands, and to other points on Nicaragua's Atlantic Coast, are handled out of a small building adjacent to the Augusto C. Sandino International Airport. The door of the building has a hand-lettered sign that exclaims:

Pliskam Pali Dor Praks
Please Close the Door
Por Favor Cierre la Puerta

The trilingual sign, and the ordering of the Miskito, English, and Spanish pleas, is a reminder that Nicaragua's

Atlantic Coast is ethnically and culturally Caribbean, not hispanic. Nicaragua's humid eastern lowlands make up some 40 percent of the country's territory, yet embrace only 8 percent of its population, mostly along the littoral. The people—Afro-Americans, mulattos, Indians (Miskitos, Ramas, and Sumus), and zambos (of mixed Afro-Indian descent)—look not to the west but to the east, to San Andrés (another small Caribbean isle), the Cayman Islands, Jamaica, and Florida.

This obscure region's history is comparable to that of Belize, where British entrepreneurs nibbled away at Spain's Caribbean underbelly to extract hardwoods and anything else of value. In Nicaragua, though, the British could not dominate the fiercely independent Miskitos, and therefore established a kingdom for their benefit, appointing (and of course bribing) the monarch. At the turn of the century, Managua gained formal control of the area, but the populace continued to see itself in some sense "English," and to view Nicaraguans from the Pacific disdainfully as "Spaniards." Following the decline of the British Empire, its commercial and cultural roles were filled by the United States.

The Somozas ignored the Atlantic Coast and it ignored them. While Anastasio Somoza, Jr., did keep houses in Bluefields (a large coastal town named for a Dutch pirate) and in the Corn Islands, no one paid any attention to him when he visited. He often walked around without a single bodyguard, something he would never have dared to do elsewhere in Nicaragua. His sole fan was a woman held to be crazy, or "stay-up" in the vernacular. (She has claimed for years that she is his true wife, and still pesters visitors to Great Corn with requests to deliver letters to President Somoza in Managua.) Although there was no fighting anywhere on the Atlantic side during the Sandinistas' insurrection, their 1979 victory declaration had immediate consequences for the Corn Islands. The Chinese merchants bolted, and the owners of the three local fishing companies, fearing expropriation, ordered their ships to San Andrés, Honduras, and Costa Rica. Subsequently the new government did indeed take over the packaging plant of one of the firms, and what was left of its fleet. Two small coconut oil plants and a hotel owned by an American couple were similarly confiscated. (My friends and I stayed at this hotel.)

As the regime consolidated its power, it announced that it would seek broader-based economic growth on the Atlantic Coast, and would try to mesh the hitherto "marginalized" territory into the nation as a whole. Unhappily, in practice, both the efforts to promote equitable development and the moves toward integration have disrupted the islanders' way of life. This conclusion was evident to my friends and me as we chatted with the islanders, hiked about "the bush," strolled on the beach, sat on a boat, ate a meal, or snacked on a coconut.

The most adventuresome—and risky—thing I did on the trip was to rent a boat for an excursion with my friend Brizio. We hired for a day a beat-up, twenty-five-foot boat, with a sputtering motor and a marijuana-smoking crew of two teenagers. The motor not only sputtered but sometimes died, the boat leaked, and the crew had never heard of life vests. But that was the only boat

for hire, and for four dollars a day we could not complain. Brizio and I wanted to see Little Corn Island. We
arrived after three hours. Little Corn Island is a natural
paradise, virtually unaltered by its scattered residents:
there are no roads, no stores, no schools, no officials. . . .
There are only simple houses, gardens, and fishing boats.
Life is lived *à la* Robinson Crusoe.

Aside from meandering around the island and swimming, we visited at length with a family who was distant
kin to one of our skippers. The old man told of the loss of
his only daughter—she was killed by a coconut that fell
on her head. One of the old man's burly sons recounted
how the last time he visited the mainland a bureaucrat
inquired if he had fulfilled his military service obligation.
He answered no. Asked why, he said he was not Nicaraguan. His surprised interlocutor wondered, "Where
are you from?" "Corn Island," the young man recalled
responding.

As we started back to Great Corn Island, Brizio had
the idea of snorkeling about an offshore reef. We stopped.
Brizio had brought along a mask and snorkel. He put them
on, plunked overboard, and started to putter around
the boat. Suddenly, Brizio—by then thirty feet from the
boat—yelled, "Shark! Bring the boat over, quick!"
The crew did not seem to believe Brizio and neither did
I, but since Brizio was my friend, I egged them to get the
boat over to him. He kept bobbing his head under the
water. Each time he surfaced he screamed, "Hurry!"
When we reached him, he clambered aboard so
brusquely that he badly scraped both his legs. That made
me believe his livid description of two six-foot sharks,

circling in water that was deeper than we had judged.

On the slow journey home, Brizio said nothing. I talked with our crew about all we had been eating at our hotel—lobsters. The crustaceans abound in the surrounding waters, and they—along with coconuts—are a mainstay of the islands. The state fishing company, Promar, devotes itself exclusively to catching and marketing them. Yet even with ten new fishing boats provided by Peru on credit, production is less than desired. One reason for this is that Promar, over the islanders' objections, insists on paying the fishermen it employs a set monthly wage instead of an amount based on the number of lobsters the fleet brings in, seriously weakening incentives. A second reason is the price paid to private fishermen. By law they must sell everything they trap to the government, and the rate offered has, in their view, been ridiculously low.

As if earning a livelihood at sea is not tough enough, fishermen find it hard to maintain their deteriorating boats for lack of paint and other supplies. The government office that is supposed to provide them with such materials has employees, payrolls, and nothing else. A further considerable irritant is Managua's insistence that each fisherman secure a permit before taking out a boat—even a rowboat. Initially these were issued on a daily basis; when the bureaucracy found itself inundated with paperwork, a switch was made to monthly permits. This has not changed the perception of the required document as one more instrument of state domination, to be manipulated at will.

When I was back on Great Corn Island I ascertained the status of the coconut business. Feigning thirst, I

stopped at the houses of farmers, asking them if they would sell me a coconut. By the time they got their machete, found a suitable coconut, whacked off the husk and crown—I had their story. The story was always the same.

Coconut farmers have not fared significantly better than fishermen. Shortly after the Ministry of Agricultural Development and Agrarian Reform began running the two nationalized coconut plants, the newer of them broke down, reportedly because of faulty management. The other one functions at 50 percent of capacity, in spite of an order forbidding the islands' third, and private, plant to extract oil. The situation reflects the cutback in production by the growers, who are dissatisfied with the officially imposed return on their crops, lagging periodic increases notwithstanding. For a brief period farmers were able to sell their coconuts on the mainland to private merchants at three times what the regime was paying. Then the government, realizing that the diversions were affecting the output of its own plants, summarily prohibited them.

An older producer summed up the attitude of most: "We just have to hop along." Quite a few islanders live off earnings from coconuts and have no alternative to selling their pickings. Nevertheless, practically nobody bothers to clear off underbrush or to plant coconut saplings, steps necessary to maintain yields. Fear of confiscation adds to the reluctance of farmers to exert themselves beyond collecting fallen coconuts, although one grower says that does not worry him because "the government is interested in control, which it already has."

Meanwhile, the artificial suppression of prices for Corn Island products has to be measured alongside the skyrocketing cost of nearly everything brought to Nicaragua. The government does ration some commodities—principally rice, beans, flour, and sugar—at controlled rates. But it has trouble with distribution; there has been much resistance to the idea of forming Sandinista neighborhood committees, widely used elsewhere in the country to dispense food. On the islands the committees are dismissed as "a lot of nonsense," or as a gimmick "for you to watch me and for me to watch you."

Besides the rationed items—only available on certain

days, at certain places, and in limited quantities—all goods are prohibitively expensive, or "dear" as the local people put it. Worse, many things are simply not available, such as medicines, spare parts, and building materials. Today, according to an islander, "When you want to build a house you first have to mash up an old house and use lumber that before you would only use for a pigpen."

Economic difficulties have undermined the Sandinistas' legitimacy in the Corn Islands. Nicaraguan currency is contemptuously referred to as "monkey money." The regime's self-serving explanations for the current distress—emphasizing, of course, the counterrevolution—generate little interest, let alone sympathy. People have drawn their conclusions from actions taken by inefficient and domineering officials, and from simply feeling that "nothing is right on the islands." The attitude of nearly all the locals was summed up by one man who bluntly stated: "In Managua the *comandantes* are supermen; here they are just bums."

Given this mentality, it has been impossible to implement conscription on the islands. Every time the issue of the draft is raised its prospective targets appropriate state-owned fishing ships and head for San Andrés, Costa Rica, Honduras, and, in one instance, Jamaica. Thus far every boat has been recovered, at high expense. Consequently, an unspoken agreement has been reached: the government will no longer try to draft the islands' youths and they will no longer steal its fleet.

Strong loyalties to the Islands have not been enough to prevent roughly half the original residents from finding the hardships so unbearable that they have emigrated. Many do not bother to get a passport and visa; they just slip away to join relatives or friends elsewhere in the Caribbean, often in eastern Honduras and Costa Rica. The Corns' population has remained stable only because residents of Nicaragua's mainland Atlantic Coast, notably Miskito Indians, have come over to escape the fighting in that area.

Those islanders who have stayed are convinced that present conditions cannot last, that something must happen. An old-timer explained: "The government is like a stretched rubber band that is going to snap. You do not know when it is going to snap, though, or which end will be the longest."

In Nicaragua's populous Pacific region, the Sandinistas derive support from their having prevailed in the prolonged struggle against the hated, old order. To the inhabitants of the Corn Islands and their brethren on the Atlantic Coast, though, Somoza's overthrow meant nothing. All the Revolution gave them was economic difficulties, accompanied by the promise of a better time to come—and they have seen no evidence to date that Managua can deliver.

The Sandinistas' ideology and development strategy call for state management of the "commanding heights of the economy" and extensive regulation of the private sector. Experience suggests to the Corn Islanders that this policy threatens the welfare of their former paradise in three ways: First, overzealous efforts to extract "surplus profits"—applied to the poor as well as the prosperous—undermine incentive. Second, the meddling of clumsy and ill-trained officials is a continuous source of annoyance. Third, an inept and burgeoning bureaucracy consumes the resources that the state extracts, with only paltry sums and benefits finding their way back to the islanders.

The government, aware of this assessment and of the resulting discontent, has sought to win islanders' support. A small health post has been constructed, inefficient electricity plants are subsidized, and transportation linking the islands to the capital has been improved. But Managua lacks the resources to reverse the downward spiral of the quality of life, at least in the immediate future.

Perhaps of greatest potential importance in these circumstances would be a government promise to grant the entire Atlantic Coast increased autonomy. Nothing would please the residents of the Corn Islands more. An articulate young woman captured the essence of the situation when she commented ironically, "The Sandinistas want to liberate us, but we are too independent to be liberated."

Walking with the Avocados

NICARAGUAN SPANISH IS DISTINGUISHED by the languid fashion in which it is spoken, by the custom of dropping any "s" that falls at the end of a word, and by the ubiquitous use of *va pues,* pronounced *va pue* (the translation of which is thorny; it does not mean anything literally, only something akin to "alright then"). Like other Central Americans, Nicaraguans love to chat and always have something to say. If they are momentarily without words during a conversation they say, "*sí, pue*" (yes, then). But Nicaraguans, or Nicas as they sometimes call themselves, are fond of paring away unnecessary words. Commonly, for example, *buenos días* is just *buenas.*

Nicaraguan Spanish is enriched by the close association of national life to the drama of peasant life in the tropics. If Bedouins have one hundred words for camel, and Eskimos one hundred words for snow, Spanish-speaking Nicaraguans have one hundred words for machete. (English-speaking blacks on the Atlantic Coast use the word cutlass, recalling the days when the region was the home of pirates.) There is even a word for someone getting sliced up by someone else (who is usually drunk) savagely wielding a machete, a *machetazo*. The names of plants and trees, of bugs and birds, are numerous and well known. The earth is close.

When something is wonderful, strong, and robust, Nicaraguans say it is *búfalo* (buffalo). Straddling the fence is *gallo-gallina* (rooster-hen). Fertilized eggs are love eggs. In Nicaraguan slang, shirt, trousers, and shoes become, respectively, cross, horse, and horns (of the kind found on cattle). A dunce is a burro; someone smart has a "good coconut." Braggarts are dismissed for thinking they are "Tarzan's mother." Children, especially one's own, are affectionately referred to as monkeys. The two heroes of children's fables are clever Uncle Rabbit and dim-witted Uncle Coyote. Some fruits, conspicuously bananas and papayas, are used as sexual metaphors (avocados are an aphrodisiac). A handsome fellow is a mango.

Many expressions and proverbs are rendered in tropical metaphor. Someone who has his head in the clouds "walks with the avocados." The idea that everyone can make a mistake is expressed as "Even the best monkey occasionally drops a zapote." The caution urged in the proverb "All that glitters is not gold" is suggested more modestly: "Not all grass is oregano." For a Sunday treat, it is common to prepare pork-stuffed tamales on Saturday. This custom has given rise to the proverb "Every pig has its Saturday."

Emotions are vented with a wide and imaginative repertoire of words and expressions. But there are decided favorites. Anyone or anything that is soothing is *tran-*

quilo. Those who irritate through their stupidity are *babosos,* which translates as something akin to "slimy slug." The idiocy of *babosos,* and anything stupid or just trivial, is dismissed as *babosada.* Disgust elicits, "*¡Qué barbaridad!*" (how barbarian). There is really only one expletive, readily used to express either surprise or anger: *hijo de puta* (son of a whore). There are numerous ways to say it, though. In addition to the orthodox *hijo de puta,* there are *hijueputa, jueputa,* and—for the ladies—*púchica.*

Every urban Nicaraguan knows at least a few words in English, most gleaned from American music and movies. Teenagers say, "I love you," and a sensitive soul has "feeling." Birthdays are celebrated by singing "Happy

Birthday." "Brother" is used so frequently that when I asked a Nicaraguan if the word was Spanish he said, "Of course." Nicaraguans have many words for money, some of which, such as *reales* and *plata* (silver), harken back to Spanish colonialism. The chic words, though, are "money" and "cash" (reverently pronounced kaash). Revealingly, the one English word adopted for political discourse is "show." *Barricada* has run headlines denouncing such and such as nothing more than "*un* show."

English names are common too. Williams are almost as common as Guillermos. When a newly nationalized textile firm initiated its first product, blue jeans, it was named Mr. Joe. And I remember conversing with a peasant family whose dog was named *el* Snoopy.

The English spoken on the Atlantic Coast is a creole with its diction and grammar heavily influenced by the canons of Spanish. Sometimes the way things are said is poetic: it does not get dark—night reaches you. On the Corn Islands a lot of time is saved by simply greeting people with "Alright." No need anymore to say, "Good afternoon. How are you?"

Aside from the Miskito Indians themselves, no one speaks Miskito. As the outside world, with all its gadgets, intrudes on them, they adopt many Spanish and English words, which for outsiders are the only decipherable words in their conversations. And for some reason the Miskito language never had words for numbers above ten. English numbers are used. Most curiously, Miskitos have the habit of naming their children after whatever happens to be around—or on the radio—at the time of their birth. There are said to be a number of Miskito Indians named Cassius Clay. And although I never met him, deep in the isolated department of Zelaya there supposedly lives a man named General Electric.

The Revolution has brought a few notable changes to Nicaraguans' Spanish. The Sandinistas have introduced some words into the common vocabulary, such as *vanguardia* and *militante*. Among the faithful, an important word is *cuadro* (cadre—and also in Spanish, square). It is hip to refer to the Revolution as *el proceso* (the process). Bums are now referred to as *lumpen,* and the rich are dismissed as *burgués* (from bourgeoisie). Those that emigrate are labeled *vende patria* (country sellers).

Among the uncommitted, the Sandinistas are sometimes referred to as Sandis, which sounds like the Spanish word for watermelon. You can get thrown in jail for publicly using the Miskito-derived expletive for the Sandinistas, *piricuaco.* Other than the Miskitos themselves, no one is quite sure what the term means, but the general consensus is "mad dog." The widely used term *contra* just means against; it is an abbreviation of *contrarevolucionario.* The Sandinistas often use the old nicknames of Somoza's National Guard when referring to the *contra.* The most frequent term is *bestias* (beasts). Foreign visitors sympathetic to the Revolution are called *internacionalistas* by the Sandinistas and their followers. Those in opposition call them by a newly coined name, *pacuso.* It combines the first two letters of the three parts of the body from which the visitors are said to stink.

The most widely used slogan during the insurrection was that of Sandino: *Patria Libre o Morir* (A Free Country or Death). The emergence of the counterrevolution gave rise to *No Pasarán* (They Shall Not Pass), which is painted everywhere. It is the same slogan used by the Republicans during the Spanish Civil War. The ambiguities of the revolutionary government are suggested by the contradiction between two common slogans: *Poder Popular* (Power to the People) and *Dirección Nacional Ordene* (National Directorate Order Me).

Slogans adorn government stationery and propaganda (the latter printed by an agency unabashedly named Secretaría Nacional de Propaganda y Educación Política del FSLN). Party officials and bureaucrats regularly initiate their letters and memorandums with a slogan. The addressee is referred to as *compañero* (comrade), which in speech is often abbreviated to *compa*. Letters often end with the declarative "A firm and revolutionary embrace."

Slogans attain their full resonance at demonstrations. Shouted by a crowd, they evoke goose bumps. I never was one to attend demonstrations, but I do enjoy concerts, and in Nicaragua every performance begins and ends with the belting out of a battery of slogans. Once I drove down to Managua's showpiece, the Rubén Darío Theater, to see a Chilean folk group, a survivor of Allende's Chile. The show was sold out, but an enterprising boy offered to find me a ticket if I would pay a premium. I said okay, and he dashed off. In a few minutes he returned with a ticket. I entered the theater and was seated, only to find that my assigned seat was smack in the middle of a large block of uniformed soldiers. Apparently one of them had sold his ticket for cigarette money. Once I was seated, everyone stared at me, wondering who I was. I speculated who the entering crowd thought

I might be—clearly someone very important, needing so much protection. So as not to further embarrass myself, at the beginning and end of the performance I rose with the soldiers, raised a clenched fist, and screamed such slogans as *Muerte al Imperialismo Yanqui* (Death to Yankee Imperialism).

The opposition, too, has caught on to the utility of slogans. The slogan introduced by the Sandinistas in 1987, *Aquí No Se Rinde Nadie* (No One Surrenders Here), was promptly adopted by the opposition to convey their unrelenting independence from the government. Even the embattled Catholic Church hierarchy began to announce, *Aquí No Se Rinde Nadie*.

A joke has it that the most common expression since the Sandinistas assumed power is "*no hay*" (there are none), a reference to shortages of food and other consumer goods. Prominently in short supply have been *huevos*, the Spanish word for eggs, which has the same second meaning as the word balls in English. *Comandante* Jaime Wheelock once declared in a speech, "They say that with the Revolution there are no *huevos*. Let me tell you, in Nicaragua there are *huevos!*"

Telephone Etiquette

FACE-TO-FACE, Nicaraguans are informal and gregarious with friends, acquaintances, and strangers alike. But telephone conversations are curt. Those who own phones do not rush to answer them when they ring. There is no anticipation of a pleasant surprise or good news. Phones are answered as if Nicaraguans are not accustomed to them, as if they convey only bad news, and as if the connection will be poor. And households are bounteous, lessening the chance that the person who answers will be the one called. So:

Alóó.	Hello.
¡Idiay!	Huh?
¿Quién habla?	Who's talking?
¿Qué quería?	What do you want?
¿Con quién quiere hablar?	Who do you want to talk to?
¡¿No se oye?!	I can't hear you.
¡Habla maj duro!	Talk louder.
'Pérate.	Wait.

No se vaya. ¿Oijte?	Don't go away. Did you hear?
Un momento, se va a comunicar.	Just a minute, I'll connect you.
Alóó.	Hello.

The Fox and the Feathers

SINCE ASSUMING POWER, the Sandinistas have sought to remake Nicaraguans' sense of national identity. Sandino's crusade against the Marines is eulogized, as is their own insurrection. The intent is to emphasize the heroic dimension of Nicaragua's history. The forty-year period in which the country was run by the Somozas is all but obliterated from official discourse. That epoch is embarrassing; it is when the country fit Hollywood's stereotype of the banana republic.

Understandably, though, when older Nicaraguans chat among themselves they sometimes reminisce about events and personages from this lengthy period. It always seemed to me that reminiscences center on one event—the earthquake of 1972—and on one person—Anastasio Somoza, Junior.

The earthquake which struck Managua a little after midnight of December 23, 1972, killed over 10,000 people, injured another 20,000, and left three-quarters of the city's 400,000 residents homeless. The earthquake ruptured traditions too. A minor but suggestive example: even today, people bemoan that the earthquake ended overnight the quaint practice of sitting outside in the evening. But most references to the earthquake are gruesome. I find them too disturbing to record in my memory. I only wonder at the earth's ability to bounce cars off the ground like a child's ball.

More entertaining are reminiscences of the last Somoza. Nicaraguans need no urging from the Sandinistas to dismiss the Somoza claim to political legitimacy. Their rule was hardly more than a kleptocracy. What has endured, though, is the personality of the figure who for so long dominated newspapers, radio, television, conversations, rumors, and the receiving end of jokes. What is remembered and recounted, sometimes at the oddest

moment, are his wit, his cunning, accounts of how he duped *gringos*, and the many jokes about him.

The hard-drinking dictator, describing Managua's devastating earthquake to a U.S. reporter, said, "It felt like we were ice in a cocktail mixer."

An especially corrupt colonel in the National Guard invited Somoza to a party in honor of the colonel's newly constructed home. The house was truly outlandish, obviously beyond the officer's salary. As Somoza left the party, he told the colonel, "When the fox steals a chicken he at least buries the feathers."

When Somoza was approached by two U.S. businessmen wanting to build a fishing plant on the Caribbean Coast, he consented providing he would be a partner in the enterprise. The three agreed to contribute $100,000 each in capital and to divide profits equally, but Somoza pleaded that he needed time to raise his capital contribution. After the papers were signed and the businessmen irrevocably sank their money into Nicaragua, Somoza remained elusive. When finally confronted and asked for his tardy contribution, he said, "Well, the sea, the land, the air—that has to be worth $100,000."

While some anecdotes just recall his ubiquitous presence, and others acknowledge his wit, jokes about the dictator are not as kind. A mad scientist visits a dungeon in Paris where the brains of famous people are for sale. The scientist walks down a corridor where Napoleon's brain is for sale for $10,000, Freud's for $15,000, and so forth. At the end of the hall is Anastasio Somoza's bottled brain with a price tag of one million dollars. The perplexed scientist asks, "Why is Somoza's brain so expen-

sive?" The clerk replies, "Because it has never been used."
After Somoza was smitten by a bazooka in Paraguay, he packed two suitcases and boldly strolled through the gates of heaven. St. Peter stopped him. The nervous Somoza dropped his suitcases and began to gesticulate widely as he fumbled for an explanation of why he should be allowed to stay in heaven. St. Peter was unrelenting. Entering hell, Somoza was personally greeted by the Devil, who escorted him to an orgy. In addition to voluptuous naked women, Somoza noticed heaping plates of food and innumerable bottles of his favorite whisky. Somoza exclaimed, "Why, this is the place for me!" The Devil smiled and said, "We knew you would fit in here." But then Somoza realized he had left his two suitcases in heaven. "Relax," said the Devil, "I'll send someone to fetch them." Up in heaven St. Peter was surprised to see two young devils jump over the gates. He shook his head and said to himself, "I sent that Latin American dictator to hell just half an hour ago, and already people are fleeing and trying to claim asylum here."

The Sandinistas have successfully resurrected Sandino, whose nationalism is universally admired. Nationalism is conflated with dignity. As for the last Somoza, he seems to have become similar to a character in an endless fable, one whose presence helps forge a sense of national identity and who amuses with alternating images of sinister wisdom and regal buffoonery.

But perhaps Somoza, or better put, the Somozas, have left another legacy, one more indelible and pernicious. Perhaps the dynasty has reinforced a particular conception of power in the collective *mentalité* of Nicaraguans.

I know well two politically active Nicaraguans, at opposite ends of the country's political spectrum. Our conversations are honest and searching. One is a member of the Superior Council of Private Enterprise (COSEP), the most prominent opposition organization. He once told me that the difficulty with Nicaraguans is that everyone wants to lead. All want to be chief, and none wants to be an Indian. In COSEP everyone wants to be president of the organization. Positions in the organization are supposed to be held for a year, but once someone is elected he stays for four years. It is the same outside the organization. Opposition to the Sandinistas has always been undermined by squabbles over who is going to be the leader.

The Sandinista I know best disdains COSEP, but when he speaks about the FSLN—and he necessarily does so circuitously—he also voices the same concerns about power. The FSLN is a Leninist vanguard party. It leads the masses, who are deemed unable to lead themselves because of their backwardness and the continuing predations of the domineering classes. But what is the proper distance between the FSLN and the masses? And within the FSLN itself, what checks are there on personality and the cult of personality?

Revolutionaries and reactionaries do different things with the spoils of power; of that there is no question. But in Nicaragua does there exist a longstanding predisposition to monopolize power? And does the monopolization of power, no matter how benign or noble the rationale, inevitably lead anywhere but to alienation, satire and ridicule, opposition, strife, and revindication?

What is the burden of memory and history on politics? Does it make a difference that there were three Somozas, that before them there were innumerable other *caudillos* (the Spanish word of arabic origin for dictators)? There is assuredly an autochthonous Nicaraguan culture, distinguished not just by the shared experience of living in a unique setting, but also by preferences and habits in the preparation of food, in the use of language, in gender relations, and so on. But to which niches of social organization does culture penetrate? Does it reach the most salient issue—power? Equally important, what in society is malleable and what is resilient? I still remember the haunting question of an older Nicaraguan woman with whom I discussed the Revolution: "How much can we change if we are still the same people?"

Crossing the Border

I AGREED TO SPEND the summer of 1988 working on a research project at INCAE's campus in Costa Rica. It is comfortable to live in Costa Rica, but I did not want to be without my beloved Fiat, still parked in Managua. So I made something like my tenth or eleventh trip to Nicaragua. It was strange to return knowing I was only coming to pick up my car and drive it across the border, to the tranquility of Costa Rica. Even on this trip, though, I would learn more about Nicaragua.

To take a car out of Nicaragua, even for an hour, one needs permission. The justifiable explanation is that otherwise the country would be left only with oxcarts. Since I was a foreigner, employed (if only intermittently) by an international mission, it was not terribly difficult for me to get permission. And I did not have to post a king's ransom as collateral, as Nicaraguans are ordinarily required. While I waited for the Foreign Ministry to prepare the necessary documents, I saw friends, looked around, and had my car reinsured and inspected by a highly recommended mechanic, Mario.

A year's worth of "full-coverage" insurance, issued by

an agent of the nationalized insurance company, cost in *córdobas* the equivalent of six dollars. I figured that for what it was worth, the policy was six dollars over-priced.

I offered to pay Mario in dollars, so he left all his other clients in the lurch to ready my Fiat for the formidable journey to Costa Rica. The task was not so difficult because most of the cars Nicaragua has imported since the Revolution are Russian Ladas. And the only difference between old Fiats and new Ladas is that "the Ladas' dashboard gauges are like those of a tractor." Parts for my Fiat were thus available. Mario did not say from *where*, and I did not ask. Within a couple of days, I had new spark plugs and a new fan belt, and all the car's lights mysteriously worked. My worn Bulgarian tires were replaced with an impressive East German set. And Mario did other things, deep in the bowels of the engine, that only he understood.

Since Mario was so resourceful, I asked him if he could possibly fix the car radio. It worked perfectly, but only when the motor was off. When the car was running, there was only static. One afternoon a smiling Mario announced that I had a new radio antenna. Sure enough, the old coat hanger was replaced by a new antenna. And what a new antenna! It was so large it was a bit scary— something more suitable for the police than for my dilapidated little Berlina. I suspected that it had been swiped off an army jeep. I masked my apprehension of someday having to explain to a uniformed official where the antenna came from. Smiling, I asked Mario, "So, now the radio works?"

"No, but you now have a new antenna."

My papers from the Foreign Ministry came after a
week. For once my name was spelled correctly, but my
Fiat was identified not as a 1973 model, but as a 1983. I
dreaded being held up at the border, either leaving or,
worse, returning. Could somebody accuse me of taking
out of the country a valuable 1983 Fiat and returning a
junky 1973 Fiat? I decided not to worry, and headed for
the border.

The drive south on the Pan-American Highway is
beautiful, even soothing. The countryside is all but de-
serted. Outside of Managua, Nicaragua often feels empty.
To be sure, along the highway are, depending on the altitude, coffee plantations, sugar estates, rolling hills of
sorghum, flat fields of rice, compact orchards of papaya,

and wide expanses of pasture on which cattle graze. There
are few reminders as to what decade of the twentieth
century you are in as you cut a swath through some of
Nicaragua's most productive land.

Not far from the border, a lone child, a small boy,
stood by the side of the highway with his thumb ex-
tended. Since there was no one else about to pick him
up, I stopped. He climbed in, unafraid. He was only
going a few kilometers to borrow some cooking oil from a
relative. He was eight and did not go to school anymore,

but he understood plenty. I asked him what he wanted to do when he grew up. He aspired to be a mechanic. He said farm laborers did not earn enough money to have enough to eat. I asked him what his father was. "A farm laborer." As he got out, he asked for one of my mangos. I said of course, and he took the largest one. As he walked away I noticed that he limped.

On the Nicaraguan side of the border I shuffled from office to office, presenting my papers and waiting while other papers were typed, signed, and stamped. My last point of call was with a fat man wielding an enormous register book. On the appointed line, my car's vital statistics were recorded, and I had to sign my name. I asked the official what would happen if something were to happen to my car while it was in Costa Rica, if the motor were to blow up or if the car were destroyed in a collision. He shook his head, thumped the register with his pen, and said solemnly, "The car has to come back."

On the Costa Rican side there was less paperwork, and I had to pay for this and for that.

It did not take long for me to realize that my beloved car—and by affiliation, I—were not welcome in Costa Rica. Costa Ricans, or Ticos, as they call themselves, never have been too fond of Nicaraguans. The Sandinistas have aggravated a long-standing perception of Nicaraguans as disorderly troublemakers. Costa Rica's liberal democracy is insulted by cars whose license plates proclaim, Nicaragua Libre (Free Nicaragua). The assumption is that the driver thinks Nicaragua is free and that Costa Rica is not. Worse yet if the license plate identifies the driver as being from an MI (International Mission). The crack is that MI stands for mierda importada.

Although the roots of Costa Ricans' disdain for Nicaraguans are complex, most of the current antipathy is directed at the tide of Nicaraguan refugees. Costa Rican officials claim that one out of ten people in Costa Rica is Nicaraguan. Coincidentally, it is widely held that ten percent of all Nicaraguans now reside outside of Nicaragua

—in Costa Rica, Honduras, the United States, or else-where. Whether the ubiquitous ten percent figure is accurate is questionable, but there certainly are many Nicaraguans who have abandoned their country, hoping to make a better life elsewhere. Every year their ranks grow. My friend Iván and his wife Patricia are two of the many Nicaraguans living and working in Costa Rica. Iván is unmistakably from the bourgeoisie. He is white, was educated at one of the better universities in the United States, and has all the ease and aplomb of a member of a social elite. Unlike many Nicaraguans, Iván never boasts of heroic escapades in the Nicaraguan insurrection. When I once asked him what he did during the war, he told me he had carried food to friends and acquaintances who fought in Managua's street battles. Many of these friends were killed. One tried to sneak guns and ammunition past National Guard lines. Soldiers pulled his pickup truck over immediately, and dug through the load of plantains to find his stash. He was shot on the spot. Iván and his friends concluded that there had been no breach of security: the soldiers instinctively knew that no white Nicaraguan would be driving a pickup truck loaded with plantains.

From the way Iván spoke of the insurrection, it was clear that initially he had wholeheartedly supported the Revolution. He never said what he thought of the Revolution now. The Sandinistas were never mentioned. But by leaving Nicaragua he and many others like him showed that they were disappointed. They saw no hope, no future in Nicaragua. Since Iván and his sisters had the means, they left. The perceived difficulties of life in

Nicaragua for Iván and his social counterparts are illustrated by the story Iván tells of his father's offices. His father's first office was totally destroyed in Managua's 1972 earthquake. His father reestablished his office on Managua's North Highway. That office was gutted when Somoza's Air Force bombed Managua's industrial district to spite the bourgeoisie who had turned against the irritated dictator. After the Revolution, Iván's father made plans to open an office in a sedate residential neighborhood. But the targeted property was abruptly confiscated for "security reasons" when a Sandinista *comandante* moved into an adjacent home. Iván says his father's office is now his car, which has become a disheveled filing cabinet. His father refuses to entertain any suggestion that he establish another office. Iván laughs when he tells the story, but it is surely such disrupted histories—and fortunes—that led him to abandon his natal country.

Through Iván I met many Nicaraguans living in Costa Rica, some of whom I had known in Nicaragua. The pattern was usually the same. They had left Nicaragua not so much because of the hardship, but because of the lack of certainty and hope in the future. Usually an unambitious brother stayed in Nicaragua to look after the family property and the parents. The parents always seem to stay in Nicaragua. They had already played out their lives; they were tired and set in their habits.

Iván and his brethren can be accused of having monopolized too many resources under the old regime. But precisely because they had so many advantages, especially a higher education, they have the most to give to a new Nicaragua. Yet there is no incentive for them to do so. For Nicaragua, these departed sons and daughters are a wasted resource, a lost opportunity.

When the summer drew to a close, I cleared my desk, said good-bye to Iván and other friends, packed the car, and drove off for the border. I had enjoyed my stay in Costa Rica. It had been wonderful to have my car with me. But I was always worried that something would happen to it and that I would not be able to return it to Nicaragua. I was haunted by nightmares of not being able to leave Costa Rica and reenter Nicaragua.

An hour away from the Nicaraguan border I was stopped by a mean Costa Rican policeman. Costa Rican policemen like to stand in the middle of the road and randomly stop vehicles in search of some possible infraction. I was always pulled over, thanks to my Nicaraguan license plates. As before, the officer acted like the Nicaraguan driver's license I presented was a damp handkerchief. He thrust it back at me and walked around the car.

"Turn on your lights."

I flicked on the light switch and said a quick prayer.

"Turn on your left signal."

"Turn on your right signal."

The policeman walked back to me and pointed at my outside rearview mirror. Mario had glued a piece of burnished tin where the car's original mirror once had been.

"Can you see anything with this?"

"Yes," I lied.

"Tell me the truth, can you see anything with this?"

"Yes," I lied again.

"Where are your seat belts?"

"Seat belts?"

"Yes, it is a law in Costa Rica that all cars have seat belts."

I decided to take the offensive. I referred to my car in the most contemptuous terms and said I was driving it straight to the border, and that I never, ever, would think of bringing it back to Costa Rica.

"That would be best," snickered the policeman as he waved me on to Nicaragua.

I was so relieved—and happy—to cross the border. I had been thinking that I did not care if the car died ten feet inside Nicaragua, I just wanted to get it out of Costa Rica and back home. Migration and customs authorities did not share my delight, but they did not obstruct me in the least. The Costa Ricans were glad to see me go. On the Nicaraguan side, I signed a few papers for migration and then went to find the customs official. He was dozing. Awakened, he asked me if I had a car. "Yes," I said, "The one at the other end of the lot." He signed the requisite form without getting up and said, "You are served."

To celebrate, I stopped at the first roadside fruit stand I encountered and bought three watermelons. Two of the watermelons, the car, and I made it back to Managua.

Revolution in a
Small Nation

THE SANDINISTAS FOLLOW the Cuban tradition of naming every year. Suitably, 1989 was christened in Managua: "Year of the Tenth Anniversary. The Revolution Stays!" The Sandinistas' mortal enemy—Ronald Reagan—moved out of the White House, having failed in his promise to see the ouster of the Sandinistas in his presidency. But on the tenth anniversary there was not much to celebrate other than sheer survival. Given U.S. support for the Nicaraguan counterrevolution—Reagan's "freedom fighters"—survival itself is an accomplishment. But what of the rosy expectations that abounded on July 19, 1979, when perhaps a hundred thousand Nicaraguans jammed together in front of the National Palace to celebrate Somoza's defeat? Unfortunately, those dreams of peace, prosperity, and reconciliation have been elusive.

Nicaragua paid a high price to oust Somoza. Forty-five thousand Nicaraguans died in the insurrection. The average age of those martyred was probably only sixteen, which is the average age of Nicaraguans at large. The economic costs of the Revolution were high, too.

Nicaragua had enjoyed less than three years of peace when the counterrevolution challenged the Sandinistas, who had adroitly consolidated power in the aftermath of Somoza's last flight to Miami. Perhaps another thirty thousand Nicaraguans were killed before the counterrevolution petered out in early 1988. Even before the fighting ended, a survey of urban Nicaraguans by psychologists at the Jesuit-run Central American University in Managua estimated that 27 percent of the population had had family members wounded or killed during the revolution or the counterrevolution. Given the large size of Nicaraguan families, as well as the depth and duration of armed conflict, this distressing finding is credible.

The counterrevolution was especially tragic because it was so unclear what the fighting was about to the population of the poor, marginal areas where the war was waged. Peasants and rural laborers joined the ranks of either army, but most peasants strove to avoid involvement in the conflict or, as they put it, "to take on color." Apathy was seen as the safest course; it conformed to the traditional Nicaraguan proverb, "Flies do not enter a closed mouth." All too often, though, poor rural and urban Nicaraguans, drummed into the uniform of one side or the other, or simply caught in the cross fire, became unintended victims. The ambiguity of the war, its lack of political import, and its toll, have made it a source of sorrow for Nicaraguans, even for those partisan to one side or the other. The war is ruefully viewed as nothing but "poor Nicaraguans killing poor Nicaraguans."

In addition to the hell of war, Nicaragua has been

wracked by economic disorder and decline. The pro-
liferation of conflicting data makes tracking the economy
a statistician's nightmare, but certain generally agreed-
upon trends convey an idea of what people must bear.
The country's output of goods and services (its gross do-
mestic product) has declined by a third since 1977, the
last year that the government considers to have been
"normal." Exports have fallen by half. Meanwhile, the
population has increased by perhaps as much as a third,
so that real per capita income has plummeted. The pur-
chasing power of agricultural wages—the most common
form of income in this agrarian land—has dwindled to
one-fifth its former level.

Aggravating this economic fiasco is the government's
chronic budget deficit. Fiscal shortfalls have been covered by what is called, in Managua, "inorganic emis-
sions"—a bureaucratic euphemism for the printing of
money—and the market's revenge has been debasement
of the currency.

At the beginning of the Sandinistas' rule in 1979, the
córdoba was pegged at ten to the dollar. By February 14,
1987, there were five wildly discrepant official rates of exchange, and a black-market rate of about 40,000 to the
dollar. On that day the government introduced new bills
with familiar faces but different colors, exchanging them
for the old ones at a rate of 1 to 1,000. (The country's
currency is printed in East Germany and the new bills
are dated 1985, suggesting that some such reform had
long been contemplated.)

It was hoped that the shock of shaving three zeros off
the *córdoba* would break the rhythm of Nicaragua's infla-

tion, which had reached three digits. But the government persisted in running deficits, so the dilution of the currency continued. To get an overall idea of the price spiral that has afflicted Nicaragua under the Sandinistas, it is illuminating to consider the cost of pineapples at Managua's Israel Lewites market. Before the Revolution the going rate for a pineapple was half a *córdoba*. By February of 1988, the price had risen to 20,000 *córdobas*. Although the currency reform then knocked it down to 20, it had again increased to over 60 *córdobas* by July. Thus, in nine years of Sandinista rule, the price of a pineapple, a locally grown fruit, was inflated by a factor of 120,000! By the tenth anniversary of the Nicaraguan Revolution (July 19, 1989), the price of pineapples had soared to 10,000 *córdobas*. In ten years of Sandinista rule the price of pineapples increased by a factor of twenty million!

Much of Nicaragua's economic distress can be traced to the damage and dislocations engendered by the Revolution and the counterrevolution. In recent years more than half the national budget has been devoted to defense. And just when the war ebbed, Nicaragua was hit by a devastating hurricane. On October 21 and 22, 1988, Hurricane Joan battered the country, causing extensive damage, especially on the Corn Islands and elsewhere in the Atlantic Coast region. In two days the hurricane set the economy back more than the counterrevolution managed to do in any given year.

Nonetheless, even fervent supporters of the Revolution tend to give the government low marks for its management of the economy. From the beginning, the intention of the Sandinistas was not just to reactivate the economy, but "to build a New Man through a state-led construction of socialism." The outcome has been disappointing. As one senior government official lamented: "Our economy is like a broken jukebox. We put in a coin and pushed the button for a tango. Instead we got a boogie-woogie."

The Sandinista regime has combined the traditional Latin American penchant for running government deficits and "covering" them by printing currency with dated Eastern European notions of a centrally planned economy. By itself, either of these tacks would be problematic; trying to pursue both at once has proved devastating for the private sector and the burgeoning public sector alike.

Whereas inflation demands quick price changes and agile decision making, the government, which intervenes to regulate the prices of many items, has made this impossible. Revisions in the price of sugar, for example, have involved five ministries and have required presidential approval, taking as long as six months. Price distortions have weakened incentives to produce, most notably in the case of export commodities. Revolutionary rhetoric and posturing have also weakened incentives to produce, save, and invest.

The economy has been kept from collapsing altogether by a trio of factors. Of these, the most conspicuous is foreign aid. Donations and credits from Western nations have pretty well evaporated, but the Soviet Union and its allies annually furnish Nicaragua with an estimated $500 to $600 million worth of goods, not counting arms and ammunition. This largess includes oil, agricultural and construction equipment, grains, and consumer items such as light bulbs and children's books (set in the icy tundra). The goods are delivered to the state-run distribution network, yet they commonly filter into the free market. Indeed, Soviet military jeeps can be found sporting license plates indicating that they are in private use.

Nicaragua is also blessed with fertile soil, a benign climate, and a favorable man-to-land ratio. Despite a markedly worsening diet, no one actually starves in Nicaragua.

Finally, there is the ingenuity of the Nicaraguans. Confronted with a web of obscure regulations, households employ an endless array of strategies to scrape together a living. The Sandinistas deplore petty trading and speculation, but without it Nicaragua would be considerably poorer. For instance, farmers who will not bother supplying milk to government plants will produce it to sell surreptitiously to private cheese manufacturers. No matter how vexing the situation may be, sheer desperation on the part of the poor ensures that there is at least a minimum of economic activity.

For those Nicaraguans not directly scarred by warfare, it is the country's economic boogie-woogie that has proven to be the most visible—and daunting—impact of the Revolution. It has resulted in untold hardship for individuals and families. But the Revolution has had other, less material consequences. The family, the linchpin of Nicaraguan society, has often been upset. Many families are physically divided, with one or more members having emigrated. More commonly, families are politically divided. Reactions to the intrusive Revolution, and political loyalties, are split in nearly every family, leading to acrimonious arguments and fractured relationships. Indeed, the Revolution has fathered divorces.

Social customs have also been altered. A minor casualty of the economic crisis has been the tradition of guests leaving small morsels of food on their plates to show that they were amply served. That custom has disappeared.

More consequentially, Nicaraguans' traditional graciousness and warmth has been eroded. Terms of endearment used to abound in everyday discourse: my love, my life, my heart, my heaven. The taxi driver stopping for an elderly woman was formerly likely to ask, "Where are you going, my love?" The response could well have been, "My heart, I am going to. . . ." Now, it is not only infinitely more difficult to find a taxi, but your conversation with the driver is likely to approximate the churlish New York norm. In other social encounters the pattern is all too often the same.

The benefits won with the Revolution are seemingly of a nonmaterial nature. Initially, there was improved access to social services, health, and education in particular. Perhaps access is still greater than what it was under Somoza, but the quality of health care and education has plummeted with the economic crisis. With the Sandinistas' ambitious agrarian reform, access to land by the rural poor has been enormously facilitated. And as elsewhere, land has a mystical appeal to Nicaraguan peasants. But this gain has been eroded by the generally abysmal state of the economy. Even with their new plots, Nicaraguan peasants remain painfully poor.

The most enduring gain of the Revolution has been in altered authority structures. Class divisions remain, as do hierarchies in the workplace. But the domineering hold of the upper strata of society has been irrevocably rocked. Gone now are their invidious comparisons and ostentatious displays of wealth, both of which long insulted the poor. For example, each private school used to have its own uniform for pupils. Predictably, prestige was accorded to those who wore the outfits of coveted schools. Private schools have survived the Revolution, but by decree all children now wear the same uniform to the nation's public and private classrooms.

More important, now everyone is treated with respect, no matter what their social status. Servile expressions, such as *a la orden* (at your service), have disappeared. In both private and public settings, workers are asked, not told, to do something. And grave violations of workers' rights, or more broadly, assaults on human dignity, are a rarity. Indeed, the erosion of authority has gone so far that in some instances, workers announce what they will do and what they will not do. Or they drag their feet (or just go home) without fear of employer recourse.

The flip side of this gain for everyday Nicaraguans has been the decline in labor productivity and the effect of this decline in retarding economic recovery. Nicaragua's beleaguered private sector agrees, but faults the anarchy of the government for the decline in worker productivity. A joke illuminates how many Nicaraguans, those most likely accused of foot dragging, see the issue: A poor Nicaraguan appears before St. Peter for judgment. St. Peter tells the man that because of his sins he will go to hell, but that he may choose either the capitalist hell or the communist hell. The frightened Nicaraguan asks, "What is the difference between the two?" St. Peter replies, "They are about the same. Both consist of getting thrown into vats where you have to eat manure. Every time you come up for a gasp of breath, someone hits you over the head with a club." The doomed man asks, "Well, which do you recommend?" St. Peter thinks for a minute and then says, "It's better to go to the communist hell. Sometimes they lose the clubs or run out of manure."

After a decade, the Revolution looks like a "bad deal." The costs have been so high, and the benefits so paltry. Yet who could dispute that it was necessary to overthrow Somoza, the greedy dictator who once boasted, "Nicaragua is not my country; it's my business." And surely the Sandinista's intention to redistribute wealth and opportunity was noble, worthy of a chance.

Ten weary years are a formidable part of any individual's life. But in the history of a nation they are nothing. Perhaps Nicaragua just got off to a bad start on the right road. Perhaps the payoffs of the Revolution are in the distant future. Maybe. As an astute Nicaraguan suggested, "Despite all the problems and contradictions, a seed of egalitarianism has been planted." He is right; that seed has been planted.

At this juncture, though, it appears that in small poor countries like those of Central America, the potential for revolutionary change is limited. What is seemingly possible is an old-fashioned smashing of privilege and a quick redistribution of wealth and opportunity. The have-nots grab what the haves have—and then as soon as possible return to the rhythms of life. But shattering the international order, challenging the world economy, constructing "scientific socialism," or building a New Man . . . these grandiose endeavors just seem to generate too much opposition and, in any case, to be beyond the managerial capacity of even virtuous governors.

Nearly every Nicaraguan accepts the Sandinista assertion that the Revolution is irrevocable. Yet after more than a decade of revolution, counterrevolution, and economic crisis, Nicaraguans display little interest in politics. People go on with their everyday lives, in part out of sheer necessity, but also as a form of prosaic resistance to the ruination of political strife. If called upon to reflect about Nicaragua, they are wont just to say, *"Nicaragua ha sufrido mucho"* (Nicaragua has suffered a lot). If pressed for an explanation, they recount the trauma of colonization, innumerable civil wars, foreign intervention, Somoza's dictatorship, revolution, counterrevolution, and, through it all, periodic earthquakes, volcanic eruptions, hurricanes, and economic crises.

The country's great drama, *el Güegüence*, offers a clue to Nicaraguans' indefatigable ability to carry forth—and in good humor no less. *El Güegüence* consists of folkloric dances in which Indians ridicule and satirize the Spanish *conquistadores*. The drama, dating to the sixteenth century, captures Nicaraguans' idiosyncracy, their cultural propensity to satirize problems and life itself. This fortifying attitude is captured by the proverb *"No hay mal que dure cien años, ni cuerpo que lo resista"* (no evil lasts for over one hundred years, and no one lives that long anyway). The outlook behind that proverb helps explain why this morning, when I asked the old woman who had served me breakfast in her humble *ranchito* how she and her family were getting along, she smiled and said, *"Aquí vamos, poco a poco"* (Here, we go forward, little by little).

Post Scriptum

ON FEBRUARY 25, 1990, Nicaraguans voted in their country's first broadly contested elections since 1921. Former U.S. President Jimmy Carter, serving as an observer, described the mood at the polls: "It's very solemn, like a Mass."

To their disbelief, the Sandinistas lost. Violeta Barrios de Chamorro, publisher of *La Prensa*, defeated *Comandante de la Revolución* Daniel Ortega. She garnered 55 percent of the vote; Ortega received 41 percent; the candidates of small parties received the remainder of the ballots. An epoch has ended, but the changes it ushered in have irrevocably altered Nicaragua.

I am sure *el Güegüence* will before long confront new, swollen political pretensions. These it will no doubt digest successfully, and emerge triumphantly with an enlarged repertoire of satire. *El Güegüence* devours all.